CONVERSION
AND
THE ENNEAGRAM
Transformation of the Self in Christ

by

Bernard Tickerhoof, T.O.R.

Dimension Books, Inc.
Denville, New Jersey 07834

ISBN   0-87193-275-X

Nothing Contrary to Faith: Rev. Christian Oravec, T.O.R., S.T.D.
Approved: Very Rev. Dennis Sullivan, T.O.R.
            Minister Provincial

ACKNOWLEDGEMENTS

For the most part, the many scripture passages quoted in this book have been taken from *The New American Bible; With Revised New Testament* (Confraternity of Christian Doctrine Edition). Any changes in the text that I have made have been either for the sake of making the passage's language more inclusive or to emphasize a particular connotation of the original biblical languages not apparent in that edition. To the best of my knowledge I have done this without in any way changing the substance or meaning of the passage.

I wish to express my deepest thanks to many people who have in various ways enabled this book to come into being. First, I thank my family, and especially my parents, who provided me with the essentials out of which to fashion a life, a vocation, and a ministry. Second, I wish to thank those who were directly involved in this book's evolution -- Fr. David Kraeger and Fr. Peter Lyons, who helped me to clarify my theological expression, and especially Ms. Susan Burke, who spent hour upon hour in careful editing of the text. Finally, I wish to thank all of those who really provided the experiential backbone of this work, the hundreds and hundreds of people who over the past decade have honestly, and sometimes painfully, shared their deepest lived experiences during workshops, retreats, and spiritual direction. Their tenacious longing for conversion and holiness have provided the truest witness to me of the Spirit's presence in the Church.

TABLE OF CONTENTS

INTRODUCTION

This book brings together two subjects that have been of primary interest to me over the last decade, a theology of conversion and the model of transformation known as the Enneagram. From my earliest days of studying the Enneagram in the autumn of 1978, the two topics seemed to me to be closely connected, although I believe at first I sensed this primarily at an unthematic level. While in some ways I presumed the link between the two, when I began to give workshops on the Enneagram I was often surprised that, although the participants seemed enthusiastic about the information they received, there were often many questions as to what they were supposed to do with it beyond the workshop. These questions led me to the conclusion that a clearer connection between the Enneagram model and the process of conversion and transformation had to be presented. The participants' response to this in the workshops, in turn, reinforced my own developing belief that some kind of further work linking the two needed to be attempted.

My interest in a theology of conversion predates my familiarity with the Enneagram system and is rooted in Franciscan spirituality. Through the 1970s, as we Franciscans sought to identify and understand our spiritual legacy of the centuries, we were continuously brought back to the sense of Francis of Assisi as a man of conversion, one inspired by the love of God to seek biblical penance. Francis' own journey of conversion greatly affected me and countless other Franciscans, religious and secular, and motivated us to

1

seek ways of recapturing the scriptural base for understanding how we today are still called to an ongoing conversion. Within my own branch of the Franciscan family, consisting as it does of both religious and secular men and women, and associated historically with the ancient Order of Penance in the Church, there has been a flurry of scholarship and pastoral activity around developing contemporary approaches to conversion and reconciliation.

One result of this focus on conversion was the realization of how far the common understanding of concepts like penance, sin, and conversion have drifted from their biblical roots. Perhaps the biggest hurdle we Franciscans have had to face in the last two decades has been the resistance to ownership of a charism of penance and conversion, after spending the previous decade trying to get beyond the aberrations of an asceticism that justified itself in those terms. The process has often been painful, but it has produced rich fruits. It has also brought home the realization that a deeper understanding of conversion is a valuable goal for contemporary Christianity as a whole.

Speaking from within the Roman Catholic tradition, this can be no more obvious than in the contemporary state of the sacrament of reconciliation. It is certainly no secret that what was, and still is, referred to as confession exists in an atmosphere of great confusion in today's Church. Partly because the catechesis on the new rite of reconciliation was not done particularly well, partly because the baggage of the past has been hard to let go of, and partly because of an uneven experience of pastoral practice, many

Catholics are at a loss as to what to make of the sacrament in their lives. Many still feel intuitively that there is something of great importance here, but their experience often leaves them feeling dissatisfied and vaguely cheated.

Beyond the Roman tradition, there is a hunger in Christianity in general for a way of making sense of our beliefs and values in a world that sometimes seems hostile and at other times feels far too comfortable. It strikes many as strange that in the midst of general affluence there are so few people who truly experience happiness and peace. There is a tangible flood of longings and desires and passions in our society, but there is also the lingering suspicion that much of the desire is misplaced. Many have turned to the human sciences for a possible answer, and while, in general, psychology and other social sciences have been tremendously helpful in providing good frameworks for understanding the problems of life, many have come away still feeling the lack of a true faith structure upon which to base their new insights.

Other Christians have seemed to forsake any hope that human insight could offer a solution, and have retrenched to a more fundamentalist position relative to their own beliefs and their experience of the world. Psychology and the human sciences do not have the answer; Jesus is the answer, the Bible is the answer. Not meaning to take anything away from well-intentioned faith, I feel this response nevertheless remains inadequate. Indeed, it is based on several false assumptions. Jesus and human knowledge are not incompatible; the Bible and science are not enemies. Nor can I read the Bible *without* a psychology. If I lack a well developed and tested contemporary psychology, I will read it with the psychology of first-century Greek and Hebrew thought, which I might find difficult to understand or appreciate, being myself a product of *this* century; or still more likely I will read it with *my own* untested and prejudicial assumptions about human life. Fundamentalist positioning all too easily becomes the safe harbor for attitudes of fear and mistrust. As believers in a scripture that tells us hundreds of times not to be afraid, we are called to recognize a basic trust in life and an essential affirmation of it.

Throughout human history many good paradigms and models of wholeness and holiness have been developed by the spiritual and psychological sciences. Some have served their purpose and passed from the scene. Others have withstood the test of time and continue to offer contemporary devotees ways of pursuing life and truth and love. One of these paradigms is the Enneagram, an apparently ancient model of human spirituality and growth. While its historical roots are open to some speculation, it certainly has caused a great deal of interest in contemporary circles. I have been studying and using the Enneagram for a dozen years, and have found it one of the most revealing and challenging growth processes I have yet encountered. But having said that, still I never expected to write anything on it.

In my initial exposure I was instructed to respect its oral tradition and interpersonal medium; it was not to be written down. To write about it would only serve to destroy its complex nuances, and freeze human experience in conceptualization. Therefore, for years I resisted writing anything on the subject, and continued to resist it even after books on the Enneagram began to appear. Being familiar with the published literature, I want to state that the initial warnings were correct. No book can hope to completely present the Enneagram. Each one has innate limitations in helping people identify themselves within the system, and some can be absolutely confusing. The best method to learn the system is still a one-on-one instruction from someone who knows both the system and the individual well. Short of that, the least that is necessary is some kind of oral instruction, such as workshops or classes, where questions can be asked and clarifications sought.

This book does not seek to be an aid in the individual's identification of a life position within the Enneagram model. Instead, it seeks to answer a need for a more complete theological reflection on the Enneagram out of the Christian tradition. It presumes a basic understanding by the reader of the Enneagram model. It therefore is not intended to stand alone as an introduction to the system. It is meant to supplement instruction and individual work on the Enneagram model of growth and spirituality, and to be a theological companion to the other literature in print. It is also intended to offer some helpful reflections on Christian conversion in light of an understanding of this ancient tool.

To accomplish this, the following material is presented in four parts. The first part of the book focuses on the teachings of Jesus, particularly as a proclamation of the Reign of God and a call for conversion. Secondly, I will present how the Christian community received this call, and how it developed historically in the Church's experience. In the third part of the book I will present the Enneagram, not only as a model of personality and a tool for self-knowledge, but also as a process for transformation and liberation. In the final section I will offer some practical considerations for the spiritual journey in light of conversion and the Enneagram.

ONE

THE TEACHINGS OF JESUS

THE STORY

Once upon a time Jesus told his listeners this parable. " There was a landowner who planted a vineyard, put a hedge around it, dug a wine press in it, and built a tower. Then he leased it to tenants and went on a journey. When vintage time drew near, he sent his servants to the tenants to obtain his produce. But the tenants seized the servants, beating one, killing another, and stoning a third. Again he sent even more servants, but they treated them in the same way. Finally, he sent his son to them, thinking, 'They will respect my son.' But when the tenants saw the son, they said to one another, 'This is the heir. Come, let us kill him and acquire his inheritance.' They seized him, threw him out of the vineyard, and killed him. What will the owner of the vineyard do to those tenants when he comes? "

They answered him, " He will put those wretched ones to a wretched end and lease his vineyard to others who will give him the produce at the proper times."

And Jesus responded, " Yes, but the son, who still lives, loved those tenants, and asked the landowner to forgive them. What do you think they will do if they get another chance? "

(Based on Mt 21:33-41)

7

JESUS PRESENT AND JESUS IN HISTORY

"And behold, I am with you always, until the end of the age." (Mt. 28:20) Thus the Gospel of Matthew ends with a promise of presence, a promise meant to inspire confidence in the Christian disciple, witnessing to the Resurrection of Christ and the sending of the Spirit. This promise of Jesus is both a consolation and a challenge. We are consoled, especially in times of personal grief or distress or in times of social upheaval and oppression, to know that the Resurrected Lord is still in the midst of his suffering people rather than blissfully resting in a distant heaven of unconcerned tranquility. It is, however, also an ongoing challenge to the faith community to continuously sort through the disheveled array of our present experiences, and seek to find once again how Jesus still lives within the mess and still calls us to embrace the life he offers.

To find the Lord present in our world is the task of all believers. It is given to poets and storytellers, to artists and scientists, yes, even to theologians. It is given to each man and woman walking on a journey of faith. Where is the Spirit of Jesus in this event? What does my faithful following of the Gospel call me to? How can I reflect theologically -- how can I "study God" -- through my everyday experiences? These are common questions of discernment that occupy our faith journey moment by moment. They are questions that spring from the belief that Jesus is not only alive but also present around us and within us at all times.

This stance of faith, however, has always caused believers to look around their world, filled as it is so often with hatred, fear, oppression, and manipulation, and conclude that the Jesus of the present, risen though he may be, is often as little understood and as little followed as he was during his earthly ministry. Just as so many who heard the preaching of Jesus either found it too hard to accept, too uncomfortable to implement, or too threatening to tolerate, many in our own world, confronted with the Gospel of Jesus today, do what seems so easy for our human nature. They again crucify the Lord of Glory.

Writers have known and witnessed to this phenomenon for a long time. In the last century the Russian novelist Feodor Dostoevsky related the story of the Grand Inquisitor in his book *The Brothers Karamazov.* Christ returned, only to find himself before the Inquisition, recognized but once more rejected. In our own day Joseph F. Girzone's story *Joshua* portrays a Christ once again walking in our midst, whose love and innocence make him the target of hatred, bitterness, and fear. It gives us sobering pause to reflect that for these more recent "appearances" of Jesus, as for their prototype, the actual earthly ministry of Jesus, it is so commonly the religious people who seem to be the most threatened, indeed who seem to have the most to lose.

It's not that we religious folk don't want Jesus around. The opposite is quite the case. We want to believe that the Risen Christ is close, but to be perfectly honest, we also want to pick our Christ. There is a subtle tendency in us to make Jesus into someone we do not have to "stretch" to know. There is a shadowy part of us somewhere that thinks it was really very nice of Jesus to go to the trouble of Incarnation, especially since we really hadn't asked or anything. Even better, the Resurrection seems to have solved the remaining problems, and since the Spirit was sent we feel rather special. If, after all that, we can't say God is on our side, and feel some confidence about it, then what was it all for anyway?

The amazing thing is, there is a part of this scenario that is true. We are a "special possession" of God, undeservedly saved, and confident in the enduring presence of God's Spirit. But, of course, it is the attitude that makes all the difference. When I -- or my group, or my community, or my denomination, or whatever social entity I make an identification with -- become the sole interpreter of the Spirit's revelation, I run a great risk. Instead of working for Jesus and the Reign of God, I am tempted to let my image of Jesus work for me. I am tempted to approach Jesus with "vested interest." Suddenly it begins to sound like my gospel, which coincidentally seems to fit my life and all too comfortably supports my values.

This self-serving attitude toward Christ (which it is important to remember we all possess to some extent) leaves out one major fact about our Savior. That is, Jesus has always challenged humanity, and Jesus continues to challenge it. The conclusive testimony of Scripture and of the ongoing Christian tradition is that Jesus challenged *everybody.* He made demands on the Twelve, he pressed the limits of commitment on his disciples, he undermined the self-centered positioning of the scribes and Pharisees. Through the gospels and the witnessing of conscience by Christian prophets through the ages, Jesus continues to challenge and question the presuppositions we Christians make about life, morality, forgiveness, redemption, and so forth. Jesus challenges our presuppositions even when we use his name to justify our righteousness.

If we are so prone to cloud our own motives and behaviors so as not to see or hear this challenge, and to actually seek to muster the forces of our salvation to frustrate our own conversion, what can we do to guard against this insidious tendency on our part? Actually, much of this book is an attempt to address this question, a question Paul painfully understood and anguished over in his letter to the Romans. "What I do, I do not understand. For I do not do what I want, but I do what I hate." (Rom 7:15) For Paul the context of his struggle was seeking to understand how it is possible for us to take "the right thing to do," which he understood as the Law, and turn it into something sinful. We ourselves squirm a bit under the thought because it hits a little too close to home.

But for the moment let us hold to the present context of the question for us: how are we to experience and understand the Risen Christ in our everyday lives without turning Jesus into some self-serving image? If the ultimate answer lies in the conversion process, and if that is the purpose of this book, then we need one practical place to start. And that is to use the very testimony of the gospels as the measure of our image of Jesus. All that we know about Jesus through revelation comes from scripture, and practically all that we know about the person of Jesus comes from the gospels. We might wish it were more. We might regret that people living in the first century did not have our inclination toward historical detail. Yet the four gospels present a very consistent portrait, or series of portraits, about this man, and what they lack in detail they make up in depth.

Modern scholarship has sought to distinguish between the Jesus of history and the Christ of faith, certainly not as two realities but as two separate methodologies in approaching Christology.[1] While it must be understood that there is not a single passage in the New Testament that does not presume the experience of Resurrection, it is also necessary to see that Jesus existed as a real human being in real historical circumstances. It must be recognized that he had a particular life, in a particular place, at a particular time, with a distinctive grouping of relationships. It must be acknowledged that these factors had as great an impact on his human development as our circumstances do on us. His cultural background, his racial and ethnic roots, his religious outlook, his language, and his field of experience all contributed to how Jesus understood his life and how he manifested his divinity through it.

Whereas this might seem obvious to many, it still meets with a great deal of resistance from some

---

[1] This can most clearly be seen in the two volumes on Christology written by Edward Schillebeeckx, *Jesus: An Experiment in Christology* and *Christ: The Experience of Jesus the Lord*, published by Seabury Press, 1979 and 1980.

Christians who harbor the feeling that Jesus was really God wearing the covering of humanity. Heretical as this position might be, it still makes its way into some of the unexpressed religious sentiment in the Church. It is for some, I feel, easier to make black and white statements concerning an omnipotent and unquestionable God than to deal with the never-ending amount of gray that sometimes surrounds our discernment when we meet a God who cares enough about us to totally embrace our humanity in both its strengths and weaknesses.

When we seek the Jesus of history there are, of course, many scriptural problems. The quest for the historical Jesus has, after all, been *the* biblical question of the last century. To lay this out before the reader is certainly beyond the intended scope of this book. But without feeling the need to go into the extensive scholarship around the historical Jesus, we can, I feel, point out something very valuable that lies right before us in the gospels as a whole. We can very simply recognize how Jesus came.

It has occurred to me on occasion that one of the abiding frustrations within the Church is our inability to cope with the realization that Jesus came among us as a first-century Semitic teacher/storyteller, and not as a thirteenth-century scholastic philosopher. In our Western mentality we long for a God who speaks "our language," the abstract language of absolute rationality. What can we do with a Jesus who seems content to make a certain point to a certain audience one day, even exaggerating the point for emphasis, and then turns around and apparently reverses himself when another situation calls for it.

What can we do with a Jesus who wants to give us peace, but who is quick to remind us that it is not peace but the sword that the disciple should expect. Can we not expect a bit more logic from our Source of salvation?

The storyteller, of course, is vitally concerned with truth, but not with the truth of dry logic. Instead the story deals with mythic truth, the truth upon which belief is based, a universal truth, but one that can concretely be applied to the specific circumstance. The storyteller's truth is one that uses human experience as its medium and not deductive reasoning. Jesus is not always logical, or even fair. Consider for a moment all the impassioned homilies we have heard "in defense of Martha," who after all seems to be getting such a raw deal to the benefit of Mary. (Lk 10:38-42) Or consider the laborers in the vineyard (Mt 20:1-16), who are not asking anything more from the owner of the vineyard than any contemporary laborer would expect.

Jesus, the storyteller, is not always logical, but he is always consistent. He is consistent because there is one truth that must be clearly and decisively stated. This truth lies at the very heart of everything Jesus says and does. It forms the very fabric of his ministry, of his life. It cannot be abrogated or mitigated. Jesus is consistent about the Reign of God, and it is to the Reign of God that we must first turn to understand conversion in the teachings of Jesus.

THE REIGN OF GOD

Imagine, if you will, turning on your television to a Christian station, and there is Jesus. The network has given him some air time to preach his message. Imagine that midway through the broadcast he begins his pitch for funds to enable him to keep his ministry going. Imagine you go to your mailbox and there among today's junk mail is the latest newsletter from Jesus of Nazareth asking for an annual pledge, pages of information detailing the wonderful healings and exorcisms and the need for your help so that it can all continue. Does it all sound a little ludicrous? Certainly Jesus had his financial supporters. We know from John's gospel that Judas held the common purse. But the idea of Jesus pitching himself and his ministry is something that the general tenor of the gospels makes unthinkable.

But if Jesus did not preach himself and his ministry, he was impassioned in his preaching of the Kingdom. In fact, of all the things that Jesus said and all the actions he performed in his earthly ministry, the preaching of the Kingdom or the Reign of God by all appearances seems to be far and above the most important. It is the core of his teaching. In Mark's gospel it is the focus of the very first thing Jesus proclaims. "This is the time of fulfillment. The Kingdom of God is at hand. Repent and believe in the gospel." (Mk 1:15) In Matthew he likens it to a treasure hidden in a field or a pearl of great price, something worth selling everything one has in order to possess. (Mt. 13:44-46)

What is this Reign of God that Jesus preaches? In one sense it is never defined, as if to name it would be to risk losing it. All that can be done is to describe it, to show the effect of its presence, and to point out what it is *not.* It is not, for instance, a territory or government. It is not what we would understand as a church or religious structure. Jesus seeks neither to establish political control nor to create a sacral organization. It is not simply the ultimate conclusion of things, the last judgment, nor is it meant to be facilely understood as a substitute word for heaven or paradise.

The Reign of God is described by Jesus most completely through story, especially through a particular kind of story known as parable. Parable is a story that reveals even as it keeps veiled, a contradiction, to be sure. It leads the hearers on until they themselves have been drawn into the story, to their benefit, or possibly, for the hardened of heart, only to find their position undermined. When asked by his disciples why he used parables to describe the Reign, Jesus answered, "Because knowledge of the mysteries of the kingdom of heaven has been granted to you, but to them it has not been granted. To anyone who has, more will be given and one will grow rich; from anyone who has not, even what one has will be taken away." (Mt 13:11-12) The Reign is proclaimed, but not all hear it; it is right here, but not all perceive it.

In Chapter 13 of Matthew's gospel the evangelist lays out for us a series of parables describing the Reign of God. It is like a mustard seed whose beginnings are imperceptible, but whose end result is strong and useful (vs. 31-32). It is like yeast, at first unobservable, but the effect of which is undeniable (vs. 33). As stated already, it is like a great treasure which must be captured (vs. 44), like a precious gem one would want to purchase (vs. 45-46). It is also like a net thrown into the sea which collects all sorts of things, which then must be discerned (vs. 47-48). Each image suggests a new insight into the Reign, but we are still left with its essential mystery.

At the risk of doing what Jesus would not do, how then can we understand the Reign of God? Let us speak of it then as the complete sovereignty of God existing from the beginning and continuing in existence, in history and beyond history, in the world, in society, in the human heart. In its overreaching expansiveness it supersedes everything, but it can be contained in the simplest phrase: "Your will be done on earth as in heaven." (Mt 6:10) The Reign of God is where God's will emerges. We often think of God's will as a master plan that exists somewhere not clearly known to us. For many it is like a mystical game show and we spend much of our lives trying to figure out the divine clues, but for Jesus it was always clear. God's will happens wherever the Reign of God is brought forth, and this is known by the fruitfulness of the event. This sense of fruitfulness is the clear indication of the presence of the Reign of God. "Either declare the tree good and its fruit is good, or declare the tree rotten and its fruit is rotten, for a tree is known by its fruit." (Mt 12:33)

The fruit of the Kingdom defies the standards of the world. If the world around us seems to favor the mighty and hold the rich in esteem, Jesus suggests that the Reign turns all this upside down. Contrary to the common wisdom of his day, the rich will find the greatest difficulty in trying to enter the Kingdom (Lk 18:24-25). Those who seek the esteem of others will not receive its rewards (Mt 6:1). Instead it is meant for those who are simple, those who are most child-like. When asked who is the greatest in the Kingdom of Heaven, Jesus brings a little child into the midst of the disciples and declares solemnly, "Amen, I say to you, unless you turn and become like children, you will not enter the kingdom of heaven." (Mt 18:3) For Jesus, then, the Reign is clearly about power. The irony is, however, that power is reversed. What seems to be power is really futility; what appears to be weakness is really strength. It should not be surpris-ing, therefore, that for Jesus the Reign of God has a social agenda, but it is one that is meant to turn society on its head.

This social agenda begins with the realization that in the Reign of God all will exist within right relationship. The fruitfulness of the Kingdom is manifested in harmony, peace, and freedom. This is the promise of salvation, the promise attested to in the three canticles of Mary, Zechariah, and Simeon in the first two chapters of Luke's gospel. The coming of Jesus, which inaugurates the Reign, will be a visitation, a redemption, and it will bring forth recon-ciliation with God. But it will also demonstrate the mighty arm of God where there is a lack of proper relationship. As Mary sings, the arrogant of mind and heart are dispersed, the rulers are thrown down, and instead the lowly are raised up (Lk 1:51-52).

And who are the lowly ones who will receive this blessing? In a very real and tangible way the lowly are those who have so far been denied blessing, that is, the poor, the hungry, the oppressed, and those whom society and religion have excluded. Jesus warns the chief priests and the elders, "Amen, I say to you, tax collectors and prostitutes are entering the kingdom of God before you." (Mt 21:31) It is this social agenda that is most threatening to the world, for there is only one way that those with power willingly share it, and that is in conversion. Most often those with power seek to keep it and actually try to increase it. But when relationships are righted in conversion, reconciliation, and freedom, then the fruitfulness of the Reign exists in that *all* are lowly, not in deprivation but in humility. Within the Kingdom, therefore, the lowly ones who receive the blessing ultimately can only be disciples, those who have clearly chosen to place themselves within the parameters of its power.

The Reign of God is a time of salvation and fulfillment. And this time is announced as gospel, *good news.* Jesus is essentially the one who proclaims this good news, and his proclamation is special in that it is itself the inauguration of the Reign. When Jesus preaches, teaches, heals, and reconciles, the Reign of God extends forth. The Kingdom is present in its Messenger. But Jesus in turn passes on the obligation to proclaim the Reign to those who have come to follow him, so that the good news can extend to the ends of the earth. It is an invitation, and there can be no coercion, for the Kingdom must be freely embraced. All are called, but many do not take the invitation. Jesus speaks of a man who holds a great banquet and invites many guests, but these guests have many "good" excuses. To excuse oneself from the banquet, however, has its implications, for there are many others on the highways and in the hedgerows to take their place. The banquet will be full. (Lk 14:15-24)

Finally, the Reign of God manifests itself as a process. As the mustard seed grows imperceptibly, so does the Kingdom. It is already here in the Messenger, but it is not yet here in its fullness. The Reign of God, it is said, is now but not yet. The disciples were no doubt concerned when they saw so many rejecting the message of Jesus, and even more concerned when they would witness defection within the ranks of followers. And yet from these small beginnings great fruit would come forth. What was only in the form of a promise in the earthly ministry of Jesus took on completely new meaning to them in the Resurrection.

THE LOVE OF GOD

Jesus was born into a people with a strong sense of self-definition. To be a Jew within the Roman Empire in the first century was to clearly recognize distinctions between oneself and anyone beyond the Jewish referant. It was a people with its own language, its own culture, its own customs, and most importantly its own religion. It was a people of the Temple with a focus toward Jerusalem, a people who longed for the Messiah or a messiah-like figure, invested with any number of spiritual and social expectations, but even more universally it was a people of the Covenant. It was this Covenant and the Law that accompanied it that formed the very heart of the Jewish religious experience. In his book,

Reading the Old Testament, Lawrence Boadt says that we should not underestimate the importance of the Sinai Covenant, that in a general sense all of biblical history could be called a theology of covenant.[2] In considering such a central feature within the world of Jesus' earthly ministry, it should be of interest to us just what relationship Jesus saw between the Covenant and the Reign.

To pose the question might at first seem strange, since from our Christian perspective the relationship would seem rather obvious. The coming of Jesus, the event that inaugurates the Reign, would be the fulfillment of the Covenant, the fulfillment of the promise of special blessing given by God to the nation of Israel. Moreover, in the paschal mystery, the death and resurrection of Jesus, there is the establishment of a new Covenant, a definitive Covenant which cannot be abrogated since the Word cannot " un-become" flesh and cannot undo the death that comes with life, a death that was salvific for all.

But this is a theological reflection that took time to develop within the Christian community. It gives evidence to a great deal of post-resurrection thought. To be sure, with the exception of its use within the institution narrative at the Last Supper, there is no indication in the gospels that Jesus used the language of covenant at all in his preaching, much less in terms of his own identity. Jesus, however, did preach the Reign of God from within a socio-religious culture

---

[2] Lawrence Boadt. *Reading the Old Testament.* Paulist Press, 1984. p. 174.

that understood what covenant was, and while he did not use the word in his preaching, it is evident that the two concepts were never understood by Jesus or anyone who heard him as being in conflict.

For the believing Jew the Covenant with God lay at the very heart of faith. The word itself, *berît*, originally indicated a verbal agreement between two parties, equal or otherwise, which detailed certain benefits and contained obligations binding upon them. While covenants could be of various kinds, the Covenant entered into between God and Israel was seen from the beginning to be unique. It was initiated by an act of God making contact with the people, and demonstrated from the beginning the personal involvement God intended. It was to be the source of unity between God and the people, and through it God's love would be made known, God's mercy made available. The people in turn would have certain obligations. Primary among these was to be the recognition and worship of the only God, the admission that all other gods were empty and false. By extension this would require fidelity and obedience. It also necessitated the return of love first given by God. In the words of the *shema* in Deuteronomy, "Hear, O Israel! The Lord is our God, the Lord alone! Therefore you shall love the Lord, your God, with all your heart, and with all your soul, and with all your strength." (Dt 6:4-5) The Covenant was therefore the manifestation of a relationship, this unique relationship of love between God and the people, found, chosen, and held special in God's eyes, a relationship simply yet profoundly stated again and again in the prophets: " You shall be my people, and I shall be your God. " [3]

Integrally bound with covenant was an understanding of the Law. Originally passed on as a collection of various groupings of legal instructions that came together in the books of Exodus, Leviticus, Numbers, and Deuteronomy, these legal "codes" were seen as representing the will of the God of the Covenant. To keep the Law was the way to assure fidelity to the Covenant. After the return from exile the Law, the *tôrāh*, was recognized as the result of the direct action of revelation by God, the absolute guide for daily life. Around this Law there emerged a further extension of legal opinions and interpretations known as the "oral law" and held by many (the Pharisee party, for instance) to be just as binding.

The Law was, therefore, seen as what mediated the Covenant. At its best it sought to be the complete manifestation of it, but in the objectification of the Law was hidden the seed of its distortion. To equate the Law with the Covenant was to potentially seek to confine in human terms the very heart of the relationship with God. No one, of course, understood this better than Jesus himself. Much of the criticism that he leveled against the Pharisees was directed toward their penchant for emphasizing the letter of the Law not only over its spirit, but at the expense of the humanizing quality for which it was intended.

---

[3] See: Jer 7:23; 11:4; 24:7; Ezek 11:20; 14:11; 37:28; Hos 2:25.

At the time of Jesus a Jewish teacher was measured by his understanding of the Law. It cannot be supposed that anyone who passed himself off as a teacher without an extensive understanding of both the written and the oral law would have been given any kind of credence whatsoever. The synagogues were the places where study and instruction took place, and any Jewish male had the right to speak, but not anyone could truly claim to be a teacher. Much was made of where and under whom one studied (see, for instance, Acts 22:3), and what position one took on specific controversial subjects. Jesus seemed to have no teachers, and their absence caused wonder in the hearers of Jesus. His status as teacher, however, was widely recognized by the sheer wisdom of his preaching and by an inner authority that left speechless admirers and critics alike.

This does not mean that the authority of Jesus was not challenged. The gospels record several occasions when Jesus was tested by representatives of the various groups within learned Jewish society, mostly in the hope of catching him within the intricate web of the Law. One such incident is recorded in Chapter 22 of Matthew's gospel, and it deserves our specific attention. It follows a confrontation between Jesus and the party of the Sadducees, made up mostly of the priestly elite. The Sadducees stood in general opposition to the Pharisees, which adds to the irony of the scene's futile conspiracy to trap Jesus.

When the Pharisees heard that he had silenced the Sadducees, they gathered together, and one of them (a scholar of the law) tested him by asking, "Teacher, which commandment in the law is the greatest?" He said to him, "You shall love the Lord, your God, with all your heart, with all your soul, and with all your mind. This is the greatest and the first commandment. The second is like it: You shall love your neighbor as yourself. The whole law and the prophets depend on these two commandments." (Mt 22:34-40)

While the context of the exchange differs in the parallels to this passage in Mark and Luke, the answer Jesus gives is the same. When asked to comment on the Law from within the perspective of his own teaching, Jesus offered a commandment of love. His answer goes back to the center of what it is to be in covenant with God, and that is to be within a love relationship. The very reason God found this people in the first place was to love them into being. To seek to understand the Law apart from love is not to understand it at all, for the whole Law, as well as the prophetic writings which sought to contextualize it in the history of the nation of Israel, are only manifestations of the interchange of love in divine relationship.

It could be stressed further that the greatest commandment is really two commandments. To love God with heart, mind, and strength is in likeness to loving the neighbor as oneself. The nature of love is not divisive; the reality of love does not exist in a certain quantity that must be apportioned out to all parties. To truly love God does not take away from human love. On the contrary, to love God naturally leads us into loving relationship with others, and to love others, free of violence and manipulation, is a return of the gift of love God has given us. "Give and gifts will be given to you; a good measure packed together, shaken down, and overflowing, will be poured into your lap. For the measure with which you measure will in turn be measured out to you." (Lk 6:38)

The Law understands that love is given to us as a commandment, and Jesus in turn reinforces the idea of love as a commandment of God. A commandment in the Old Testament is a "word," *dabar.* When God gives Moses the ten commandments, what he receives are *debarim*, words spoken by God. And God's word is never spoken in vain . "So shall my word be that goes forth from my mouth; it shall not return to me void, but shall do my will, achieving the end for which I sent it." (Is 55:11) Love, then, is the word God principally speaks, and we in turn must speak this word to others. This is doing God's will, which is what the Law hopes to achieve. It is also how we understand the Kingdom, where God's will is done. The Covenant and the Reign come together, therefore, in our action toward this "word" of God, this commandment of love.

The covenant love of God, like the Reign, is complete and total. On God's part there is an absolute commitment to love. While in the Old Testament God punishes transgressions of the Law, the covenant is never abandoned. In the gospels the good news of the Reign might be rejected, Jesus himself might be rejected, but there is no question of God's commitment to the process. As God's love is total and complete, so too is ours to be. We are to love God with every aspect of our being, and to let that love flow out on all things. Today we would speak of covenant love as being "holistic," not just a concept but a fully embodied experience, manifested in action, congruent in appearance, radical in scope.

It was the radical scope of the commandment to love that was perhaps its most challenging aspect for those who heard Jesus preach. In Matthew's gospel Jesus is portrayed as the new Moses, giving a new law in the Sermon on the Mount (Mt 5-7). Part of this new law deals with the radical nature of love.

> You have heard that it was said, "You shall love your neighbor and hate your enemy." But I say to you, love your enemies, and pray for those who persecute you, that you may be children of your heavenly Father, for he makes his sun rise on the bad and the good, and causes rain to fall on the just and the unjust. For if you love those who love you, what recompense will you have? Do not the tax collectors do the same? (Mt 5:43-46)

The "new law" of Jesus seeks to carry the commandment of love to its radical conclusion. It is not enough to forbid killing; even anger is liable to judgement. Retaliation is transformed into positive action toward the enemy. Judgment is rendered only at the risk of being judged in turn. And re-emphasizing the fundamental law of love Jesus tells those who listen, "Do to others whatever you would have them do to you. This is the law and the prophets." (Mt 7:12)

In John's gospel this law of love is presented as a *new* commandment. In Chapter 13, following the washing of the disciples' feet, where Jesus gives them an example that they too are to follow, he then speaks of his coming glory, that is, his death. Then he says to them, "I give you a new commandment: love one another. As I have loved you, so you also should love one another. This is how all will know that you are my disciples, if you have love for one another." (Jn 13:34-35) This radical love, then, is to be a love even to death. The nature of this love is spelled out even more clearly later in the final discourse in Chapter 15.

> This is my commandment: love one another as I love you. No one has greater love than this, to lay down one's life for one's friends. You are my friends if you do what I command you. I no longer call you slaves because a slave does not know what his master is doing. I have called you friends, because I have told you everything I have heard from my Father. It was not you who chose me, but I who chose you and appointed you to go and bear fruit that will remain, so that whatever you ask the Father in my name he may give you. This I command you: love one another. (Jn 15:12-17)

Contained within this inclusion structure of the commandment of love, the evangelist gives emphasis to the nature of the love that Jesus calls us to. It is to be a radical love even to death, the laying down of one's life. It embodies the relational love of the Covenant, which is not a relationship of slavery but of freedom, a relationship of friendship. As in the Covenant God initiated the relationship, so does Jesus choose the disciple. This disciple is then called to go forth to bear fruit, the sign of one's connectedness with Jesus, the true vine (Jn 15:4), and in the larger context of the gospels as a whole, a sign of the Reign of God.

THE CALL TO CONVERSION

The message of Jesus was to recognize the time of fulfillment, the inbreaking of the Reign of God, and to embrace the will of God in the radical relational love of the Covenant. Jesus proclaimed this message almost exclusively to the Jewish people, his own people, the people of Abraham, Moses, and David, a people who believed they were chosen in Covenant by God. But one thing was regrettably very clear about these people who sought to live within God's Covenant: from the very beginning, from the time they were led out of the land of slavery, from the very day of the Covenant, the people had entered into sin. Not only did they enter into sin, but also they continued to sin all through their wandering in the desert, in the midst of their settling of the Promised Land, and through the checkered history of their kings and leaders. Moses had pleaded with God for the people. The prophets had spoken out continuously about their idolatry, about their futile military alliances, about their flagrant social injustice. And in their moments of lucidity the people had come to understand that they had brought their own circumstances upon themselves. The fundamental sin of the people was the lack of fidelity to the Covenant with God.

The prophets had ceased to speak for a long time when John the Baptist came upon the scene, and word that a new prophet had begun to preach caused great excitement. John appears as a somewhat mysterious figure in the gospels. His message was unmistakably similar to that of Jesus. He announced the proximity of the Reign of God, and he called for a radical repentance symbolized in a ritual bath for the forgiveness of sin. John's call to repentance did not fall completely on deaf ears, and many, including Jesus and at least some of his closest disciples, had sought out this bath of renewal. John apparently had a great influence upon Jesus, an influence that the early Christian community was hard pressed to explain and, wherever possible, quick to find distance from lest Jesus be misconstrued to be a disciple of John.

John's message, however, was not exactly the same as Jesus', in emphasis as well as content. John's style of preaching was reminiscent of the Old Testament prophets, a clear and strident tone of judgment. The Reign of God was to be a day of God's wrath. "Even now the ax lies at the root of the trees. Therefore every tree that does not bear good fruit will be cut down and thrown into the fire." (Mt 3:10) Nor was there any sense that John perceived his own ministry as initiating the Reign. At least as the gospels present John, he was looking for another to come after him, and while the Reign was imminent, it was not yet here.

Where John and Jesus clearly concurred was in the urgent need for a total conversion from sin. "Produce good fruit as evidence of your repentance," John tells the Pharisees and Sadducees. (Mt 3:8) In Luke's gospel John's approach to repentance was a very practical one, offering concrete actions to those who were moved to reform (Lk 3:10-14). In all this John clearly spoke a message that was to be repeated by Jesus. While Jesus did not present the same severity of style, he was just as insistent upon the need for reform. In fact, the call to conversion was an essential part of the earliest preaching of Jesus. He saw it as an integral piece of the manifestation of the Reign, a response to its commencement (Mk 1:15). The very fact that the Kingdom of God was breaking into human reality made conversion urgent.

How are we to understand this call to repentance in the preaching of Jesus? The word that the evangelists use for repentance, conversion, or reform is the word *metanoia* (the noun) or *metanoeō* (the verb form), a fundamental internal change of attitude, a change of heart or mind. It is therefore a word that connotes some kind of interior transformation. By its use in the gospels, however, it seems clear that it is also meant to convey the sense of the Hebrew word *sûb* (pronounced "shoov"), which in the Old Testament is the word most commonly used for the action of repentance. *Sûb* designates a literal turning back, a return to a former place, a change of direction, and is used, particularly by the prophets, to convey the moral imperative to reform.

What we call the Old Testament, we sometimes forget, was the only "bible" Jesus had. His scriptural understanding of conversion, therefore, was in line with the call to repentance out of the prophetic literature. Conversion could never have been seen by Jesus as exclusively a change of mind, in the sense of being a series of new conclusions drawn from further insights and additional information. It was not merely a profession of a new political or religious position, as the word can be understood in our culture. Nor was it only a change of heart, as we might have new feelings about someone who was once an enemy but who has since been forgiven. What was stated earlier about love, and the need to understand the love to which God calls us as holistic, could similarly be said of conversion. Conversion also had to be holistic. It was to be a total and complete experience. It demanded an interior change, accompanied by a restructuring of motivations, but it also required congruent action, which both gave witness to the change and reinforced it by a new construct of behavioral patterns.

Like the prophets before him, Jesus was critical of pronouncements that gave lip service to conversion but were really self-serving statements. Real repentance required a complete personal change of life structure, which ultimately could only be measured by the fruit of one's actions. On one occasion, for example, Jesus presented to the priests and the elders the following parable:

> What is your opinion? A man had two sons.
> He came to the first and said, "Son, go out

and work in the vineyard today." He said
in reply, "I will not," but afterwards he
changed his mind and went. The man
came to the other son and gave the same
order. He said in reply, "Yes, sir," but he
did not go. Which of the two did his father's will? (Mt 21:28-31)

Jesus did not condone the first son's original
refusal to go and work in the vineyard. Nor did he
condone the lives of sin led by the prostitutes, tax
collectors, and sinners who ate and drank with him
during his ministry. Yet he detected in them a hunger
for God's word and a willingness to change the
direction of their lives. It was the kind of hypocrisy
demonstrated in the actions of the second son, hypocrisy that Jesus detected in many of the well-estab-
lished social and religious elite of his society, that
caused him the most distress and anger. It was these
people, the elders, scribes, priests, and teachers, who
were most challenged by Jesus, because he saw them
as being in most need of repentance. But ironically it
was this very attitude of hypocrisy and self-deception
that made conversion so difficult.
He tells them:

You brood of vipers, how can you say good
things when you are evil? For from the
fullness of the heart the mouth speaks. A
good person brings forth good out of a
store of goodness, but an evil person brings
forth evil out of a store of evil. I tell you,
on the day of judgment people will render

an account for every careless word they speak. By your words you will be acquitted, and by your words you will be condemned. (Mt 12:34-37)

Resistance to conversion ran high among those who listened to Jesus preach. This should not surprise us, since we too can be very resistive to the gospel call to conversion. Many who listened to Jesus were greatly attracted to his words, but began to seek distance from them when they realized their implications. Some, out of fear and insecurity, were all too willing to give credence to the objections of the Pharisees that he was disrespectful of the Law. Jesus was aware of their rejection, aware of their unquenchable desire for certitude before they would risk a commitment.

While still more people gathered in the crowd, he said to them, "This generation is an evil generation; it seeks a sign, but no sign will be given it, except the sign of Jonah. Just as Jonah became a sign to the Ninevites, so will the Son of Man be to this generation.... At the judgment the people of Nineveh will arise with this generation and condemn it, because at the preaching of Jonah they repented, and there is something greater than Jonah here." (Lk 11:29-30,32)

While Jesus is harsh with the kind of self-deception and fear that resists conversion, his invitation to repentance is anything but that. He accepts the individual where he or she is, and while asking a total commitment to the restructuring of one's life around the Reign, he does not get caught up in the "show" of conversion. It is better for one to make clear and permanent life changes than to assume an outward form that in reality possesses no content. "When you fast, do not look gloomy like the hypocrites. They neglect their appearance, so that they may appear to others to be fasting. Amen, I say to you, they have received their reward." (Mt 6:16) The fact that Jesus doesn't ask for harsh ascetical practices causes some controversy among those who hear him. People notice the contrast between the rigorous demands of fasting that other religious leaders place upon their followers and the relative laxity of the followers of Jesus (Mk 2:18). He himself apparently received criticism for what some considered too frivolous a social presence and behavior unbecoming a religious leader (Lk 7:34). But Jesus does not seek to justify himself, instead offering a warning to those who would use their own religious judgmentalism as an excuse for postponing repentance.

In the gospels the call to conversion is primarily a call to faith. In the passage cited from Chapter 1 of Mark, conversion and faith are linked together (Mk 1:15). It would be unthinkable to ask people to change their lives so radically without a new foundation upon which to build. This new foundation is faith, not just a faith in God, or in God's goodness revealed in Covenant, but especially faith in Jesus, the Messenger and the Message. It is revealing that the Greek words for faith, *pistis* (the noun) and *pisteuō* (the verb form), also express the concept of trust. The two English expressions need to be placed together if we are to understand what the gospels are asking of us. The faith that Jesus calls people to is not the acceptance of an idea or concept. It was the rare and exceptional resident of Judea and Galilee who didn't "believe in God." The faith that was asked by Jesus of his hearers was a faith upon which life decisions were based, a faith that could respond to the invitation to "come and follow me." It was the faith that demanded a complete and total trust in this person and what he promised.

In John's gospel a distinct conversion language is not used. Instead John uses the language of faith to completely encompass the idea of conversion. Faith is an essential feature in the fourth gospel; it is the very motive for the Word coming into the world.

> The true light, which enlightens everyone, was coming into the world. He was in the world, and the world came to be through him, but the world did not know him. He came to what was his own, but his own people did not accept him. But to those who did accept him he gave power to become children of God, to those who believe in his name, who were born not by natural generation nor by human choice nor by a human decision but of God. (Jn 1:9-13)

The fundamental question in John's gospel is: Will you believe or not? "For God so loved the world that he gave his only Son, so that everyone who believes in him might not perish but might have eternal life."(Jn 3:16) For John it is not Jesus who will condemn those who refuse to believe, for they will bring about their own condemnation.

> Whoever believes in him will not be condemned, but whoever does not believe has already been condemned, for not believing in the name of the only Son of God. And this is the verdict, that the light came into the world, but people preferred darkness to light, because their works were evil. For everyone who does wicked things hates the light and does not come toward the light, so that one's works might not be exposed. But whoever lives the truth comes to the light, so that one's works may be clearly seen as done in God. (Jn 3:18-21)

To prefer light to darkness, to come into the light and thereby live in the truth, these are the actions of conversion in John's gospel. They can only be accomplished through belief in Jesus, for it is Jesus, the Eternal Word, who came to offer this new kind of life, a life that is painted in terms of freedom. "Amen, amen, I say to you, anyone who commits sin is a slave of sin. A slave does not remain in a household forever, but a son always remains. So if a son frees you, then you will truly be free." (Jn 8:34-36) Who is the one who has this kind of freedom? Who has left behind the darkness of sin to pursue the light of conversion, faith, and truth? This is the one we have come to know as a disciple.

THE COST OF DISCIPLESHIP

From the very beginning of his ministry, Jesus called disciples. In this he was not unusual, for John as well as many of the other religious figures of the time were also open to taking on disciples, whom they instructed in their own spiritual principles. It seems, however, that Jesus was quite active in procuring disciples, actually picking out individuals he would invite to join his group. To be a disciple of Jesus, one had to take the good news of the Reign of God to heart, to make a decision of faith for Jesus, to seek conversion, and to leave behind life as one knew it in order to follow him.

The disciples of Jesus were ordinary people, possessing nothing special that would tend to single them out. They were men and women, coming from all walks of life and all professions. Some had been sinners, perhaps some were educated, possibly even coming from the highest circles of Jewish society, but most seemed to be common people. It would seem that at some point in the earthly ministry of Jesus there were twelve men singled out to be those disciples closest to Jesus, apparently picked to fulfill the role of the new patriarchs in the coming Kingdom. But the Twelve were certainly not the only disciples of Jesus, nor were they the only ones who traveled with him.

While the disciples of Jesus came from ordinary life circumstances and were in no way special in the eyes of the world, something special was certainly asked of them by Jesus. It is unlikely that any would

have remained long in their midst without a deep
commitment to the Gospel he was preaching, for to
Jesus discipleship involved a terrible cost. It was
certainly a choice the individual could make, but once
that choice was made, discipleship was complete and
absolute. "No one who sets a hand to the plow and
looks to what was left behind is fit for the kingdom of
God." (Lk 9:62)

Most of us would like to consider ourselves
disciples of Jesus. Most of us have probably made a
commitment to Jesus and the Gospel, perhaps verbal-
ly, perhaps sacramentally. We have some idea of
what the gospels ask and could at least say we are
"trying" -- sometimes! Yet just as we have a tendency
to fashion a Jesus we can comfortably live with, so
there is the temptation to create an image of the
disciple more in keeping with our current values. It
can therefore be disconcerting to realize that some of
the very things we might consider "Christian" are not,
as such, true marks of discipleship as presented by
Jesus in the gospels.

For instance, we might be led to think that a
person who professed the name of Jesus, publicly
witnessed to that name, and made great efforts to
manifest its power, would certainly be considered a
disciple of Jesus. And yet we hear Jesus say in
Matthew's gospel:

> Not everyone who says to me, "Lord, Lord,"
> will enter the kingdom of heaven, but only
> the one who does the will of my Father in
> heaven. Many will say to me on that day,
> "Lord, Lord, did we not prophesy in your

name? Did we not drive out demons in
your name? Did we not do mighty deeds
in your name?" Then I will declare to
them solemnly, "I never knew you. Depart
from me, you evildoers." (Mt 7:21-23)

So while it is true that one is *not* a disciple
because of the performance of religious acts, this
passage does give us a very clear insight into what
discipleship involves, that is, the doing of God's will.
But here we would-be disciples run into another
problem. For most of us there is a tendency to
equate doing the will of God with doing "the right
thing." Perhaps since our earliest childhood we have
been faithfully trying to discover what is right and
then carry it out. It's quite possible, therefore, that
we have been good boys and girls, but we have not
been disciples of Jesus. We need only look at the rich
young man to illustrate this.[4] In the gospel accounts
he comes not seeking discipleship as such, but eternal
life. Since his youth he has fulfilled the Law, that is,
he has kept the commandments. He has done what
is right. With this Jesus seems to be satisfied, and in
Mark's gospel, even looks upon him with love. But
the rich young man wants to do more. For that, Jesus
tells him, he must pursue discipleship. "You are
lacking in one thing. Go, sell what you have, and give
to the poor and you will have treasure in heaven; then
come, follow me." (Mk 10:21)

---

[4] Mt 19:16-22; Mk 10:17-22; Lk 18:18-23.

It is hard spending one's life doing what is right only to discover that discipleship asks for more. The rich young man goes away sad. We could say that this is when the Good News is bad news, that is, when the Gospel breaks through our comfortable beliefs and places demands on us. Many of us have spent our lives trying to be "pleasing to God," sure that this is what discipleship consists of, secretly believing that God would certainly commend us for our efforts. But Jesus offers us a parable:

> Who among you would say to your servant who has just come in from plowing or tending sheep in the field, "Come here immediately and take your place at table"? Would he not rather say to him, "Prepare something for me to eat. Put on your apron and wait on me while I eat and drink. You may eat and drink when I am finished"? Is he grateful to that servant because he did what was commanded? So should it be with you. When you have done all you have been commanded, say, "We are unprofitable servants; we have done what we were obliged to do." (Lk 17:7-10)

If public profession of the Lordship of Jesus, acting correctly, and trying to be pleasing to God are no guarantee of discipleship, what makes one a true follower of Jesus? If Jesus identifies the doing of God's will as a sign of discipleship -- God's will which we have seen situates the presence of the Reign --

then how are we to recognize it in the life of the disciple? In other words, what is the fundamental mark of the disciple of Christ? It would seem that in the gospels Jesus is inclined to link discipleship to *renunciation.*

Renunciation is not a particularly popular value in our culture. If anything, many in our society live as if renunciation is to be avoided at all cost. How could something that many tend to equate with antiquated religiosity, with some kind of ascetical aberration or unhealthy dehumanization, be the key feature of discipleship? And yet Jesus is quite clear on the matter.

> If anyone comes to me without hating father and mother, wife and children, brother and sister, and even one's own life, this one cannot be my disciple. Whoever does not carry one's own cross and come after me cannot be my disciple.... Everyone of you who does not renounce all your possessions cannot be my disciple. (Lk 14:26-27,33)

It is, unfortunately, for many just that much more bad news of the Gospel. These attachments, after all, are good things, are they not? They are by nature love commitments; they are, as it were, fulfilling the very command that Jesus gave us. How can we hate what we are supposed to love? (It is about this time that we again wish Jesus had come as a scholastic philosopher.) And what can we make of hating our own lives? Particularly in this present age of self-esteem and personal positive regard, this seems so far from what we recognize as a humanly healthy value.

Actually, it is in the very contradiction of our experience that we begin to see what Jesus is really presenting. The one who is seeking discipleship is *expected* to wrestle with the problem, one that was just as perplexing to those who heard Jesus as it is to us. This radical reversal on life is presented in an even more direct way in a passage that is recorded in every gospel account. In Matthew it appears as follows:

> Then Jesus said to his disciples, "Whoever wishes to come after me must deny oneself, take up one's cross, and follow me. For whoever wishes to save one's life will lose it, but whoever loses one's life for my sake will find it. What profit would there be for one to gain the whole world and forfeit life? Or what can one give in exchange for life?" (Mt 16:24-26) [5]

Even though the language Jesus uses is contradictory, the sense of the passage is fairly direct. In seeking to preserve what I feel is important, I run the risk of losing what is really important. In letting go of what is inessential in my life, I open myself to the awareness of what is truly essential. There are, then,

---

[5] See also: Mt 10:38-39; Mk 8:34-37; Lk 9:23-25; Jn 12:25.

in effect, two lives. There is a life that the Reign of God asks me to lose, and there is a life that I am urged to find. So at the very heart of discipleship is a discernment question. What are these two distinct lives found in my experience, and how do I act concretely in regard to them in order that the Reign of God might bear fruit?

In this passage Jesus does offer us some help in discerning an understanding of the presence of these two lives. First, it is clear that the life I am to find in the Kingdom is indeed worthy of self-esteem. Compared to having this life, gaining the whole world would be as nothing. There could be no equal rate of exchange, nothing worth the sacrifice. In this sense, the life to find is much like the Reign of God itself. It is the treasure hidden in the field, worth selling all in order to possess it, the pearl of great price. When Jesus says that the Reign of God is in our midst (Lk 17:21), there is already the sense that this life of the Kingdom is there to be discovered.

Let us consider for a moment the word for "life" in the gospels. It is a word that has many shades of meaning in the Greek. The word *psychē* can have the meaning of breath, and can therefore also represent the vital force which animates the person. As such it has the inferred meaning of life itself, as most translations render it in this passage. It can also refer to that in which life can be found, a living being. As the life's breath within the person, it can further be understood as the center of human feelings, desires, affections, and so forth, what we call the soul. It can also translate soul as a moral being seeking its highest end, as well as soul as a personal and unique essence.

It is, therefore, the word we could use for that part of each of us that is deepest and most truly myself. In that case, this discovery of incalculable worth is what could be called our *truest self,* that within us which most reflects the image and likeness of God (Gen 1:27). There is, however, the matter of the other life, the life to lose. Jesus also offers us a clue to this discernment as well. In the passage from Matthew, the renunciation of life is put in terms of carrying a cross. Whether this was simply the use by Jesus of a common dramatic image, the foresight of his own experience, or a later editing by the faith community, the sense of the image Jesus uses is very clear. Discipleship has to do with death. The parallel passage of the two lives found in John's gospel paints for us a vivid picture. "Amen, amen, I say to you, unless a grain of wheat falls to the ground and dies, it remains just a grain of wheat; but if it dies it produces much fruit. Whoever loves life loses it, and whoever hates life in this world will preserve it for eternal life." (Jn 12:24-25) The life to lose, then, is "life in this world," life prized by worldly standards, the life of self-importance, the life I seek to protect and defend, the desire to "be somebody" and the fear that I really am not. There is, then, within us a *false self* that misleads us, and distorts what is truly essential.

The disciple, then, is the one who seeks to correctly discern these two subtle understandings of self. They are not easily differentiated. Not even the closest disciples were able to clearly distinguish which was which. What starts out good can end mired in self-interest; what begins in pursuit of the Kingdom can end in the creation of one's own kingdom.

> Then James and John, the sons of Zebedee, came to him and said to him, "Teacher, we want you to do for us whatever we ask of you." He replied, "What do you wish me to do for you?" They answered him, "Grant that in your glory we may sit one at your right and the other at your left." Jesus said to them, "You do not know what you are asking. Can you drink the cup that I drink or be baptized with the baptism with which I am baptized?" They said to him, "We can." Jesus said to them, "The cup that I drink, you will drink, and with the baptism with which I am baptized, you will be baptized; but to sit at my right or at my left is not mine to give but is for those for whom it has been prepared." (Mk 10:35-40)

It is perhaps not so surprising that the others close to Jesus would protest this request, for probably they themselves had similar desires. Jesus takes the opportunity to re-emphasize the importance of humility in the Reign. "Whoever wishes to be great among you will be your servant; whoever wishes to be first among you will be the slave of all." (Mk 10:43-44) But Jesus has also placed their discipleship in the context of sharing his cup, that is, his fate. The baptism he offers them is his death, or more properly their sharing in his death by their own. Death, however, is not simply physical death or martyrdom. It is death for the sake of the Gospel. While it could mean martyrdom, as it did for most of the Twelve, it can also be seen in the context of persecution, which will predictably come to those who preach the Reign of God.

There is also an aspect of death present in renunciation itself, for the disciple must watch die all that stands as a barrier to fulfilling the will of God as it appears at that moment. The one who seeks discipleship must "hate" all that presents itself as an obstacle to the Kingdom, whether it is something outside of oneself or something within. The disciple must let such obstacles die, even if they are in themselves good, if the false self has attached itself to them in such a way that the Reign is retarded. Ultimately the disciple must let *everything* but the Kingdom fall away. "Do not be afraid any longer, little flock, for your Father is pleased to give you the kingdom. Sell your belongings and give alms. Provide money bags for yourselves that do not wear out, an inexhaustible treasure in heaven that no thief can reach nor moth destroy. For where your treasure is, there also will your heart be." (Lk 12:32-34)

THE APPROPRIATE MOMENT

The gospel of Luke records an incident in the ministry of Jesus that could at first seem to us harsh and uncaring. Jesus has resolved to go to Jerusalem, there to fulfill God's will. As he goes he sends messengers ahead of him, while he himself continues to proclaim the Reign of God. The gospel portrays several individuals who are drawn to his preaching, and want to follow him. They all, however, present certain qualifications to their discipleship. One of them, whom Luke presents as being sought out by Jesus, replies to the invitation, "Lord, let me go first and bury my father." To which Jesus replies, "Let the dead bury their dead. But you, go and proclaim the kingdom of God." (Lk 9:59-60) It is quite possible, as some suggest, that the man's father was still in relatively good health, but it is clear that Jesus doesn't stop to inquire. And if his response seems unfeeling to us, it would have literally been shocking within his own culture, which held the duties of a child to one's parents as sacred. The point that Jesus is making is evident. Discipleship is what will bring life, and its invitation is not something one can put off. The Reign of God is breaking in; it is here in the one who preaches it. There is no time to wait in accepting it or proclaiming it. One who delays will miss the opportunity. What is the source of this urgency that is so tangibly sensed in Jesus' teaching?

The preaching of Jesus, like the little we know of the preaching of John the Baptist, cannot be totally removed from the religious context of its historical setting. Both John and Jesus were born into a spiritual ambiance that understood and responded to the idea of the prophetic. Prophecy was the proclaimed word of God delivered through the mouth of the human agent. The prophet was one of the dominant forces in scripture. While not always heeded, the prophet delivered the word of God, which when tested was considered God's will. John certainly styled himself as a prophet, and the people who responded to him also perceived him in this way (Mt 11:9-10). Jesus, while never claiming a mission only as prophet, was also highly influenced in his preaching by the characteristics of the prophetic tradition. While its influence is harder to isolate, there are also strains of the apocalyptic that can be seen in the teaching of Jesus. The religious atmosphere of the Inter-Testament period just prior to the time of Jesus was dominated by apocalyptic thought. The Jewish people were surrounded by the cultural and political forces of the Greek and Roman world that were seemingly beyond their power; only God could shatter the bonds of their oppression. The apocalypticist was not a prophet but more an interpreter, one who sought to interpret a view of human history in the light of the dramatic events of an imminent end time, the eschaton (from *eschatos*, the last things). Usually apocalyptic writing took a pessimistic view of human undertakings, and held that only a direct intervention by God would set things right. It was more commonly presented through a written genre rather than through the spoken word, and was often veiled in the language of symbol and metaphor. (The word *apokalupsis* means an unveiling, where the anonymous author makes known to those who have an understanding of the symbols what will happen.)

While elements of apocalyptic thought can be seen in the eschatology of Jesus, he more evidently approaches the Reign of God out of the line of prophetic structure. Jesus is not content to interpret history, but is more intent on delivering God's definitive word of salvation. Though it seems likely that he expected a quick resolution to history, Jesus could hardly be considered pessimistic toward human endeavor. While the reality of sin and the resistance to conversion could not be denied, the hearer always had the choice of discipleship. The very preaching of the Kingdom was meant to urge his hearers to act.

How, then, are we to understand the urgency we experience in the tone of Jesus' preaching of the Reign of God? In part, the answer lies in the prophetic concept of the Day of the Lord. The term itself seems to have predated the prophets, and was originally a reference to a day of judgment that God would deliver against Israel's enemies. The Day of the Lord would be a day of victory and rejoicing. But the prophet Amos, speaking out against the sinfulness of Israel, reshaped the concept (Amos 5:18-20). Instead, it would be a day of woe, a day of darkness. It would be a day of judgment against God's own people for their faithlessness. Following this understanding of Amos, the prophets began to warn the people of the coming day of judgment, a day within history that would bring terror to those who had strayed from the ways of God. It would, however, be a day of salvation for those who had remained faithful, even if they comprised only a remnant of the nation. With the apocalyptic influence the Day of the Lord took on more cosmic and ahistorical proportions. It would be a day of cataclysmic judgment, a day when God would end the old order and definitively replace it with the new.

The preaching of Jesus must be seen within this theological development. There was a day coming, and it would be one of judgment. Its timing was known only to God. It was therefore incumbent upon

each person to prepare for its appearance by conversion (Mt 24:36-44). The early Christian community
believed, as Jesus had apparently taught, that this day
was coming soon. It would be inaugurated by the
return of the Risen Christ in glory. As the years
passed and it became increasingly more obvious that
the Day of the Lord was delaying, the Church's
theological understanding developed. Christ would
return, but it could not be known when; we were
living in the final age, but no one could be certain
how long that age would last.

But was the urgent call for discipleship in the
preaching of Jesus simply based on his belief in the
imminent coming of the Day of the Lord? The
answer, it seems, would be no. What else would be so
pressing that it would allow for no delay in responding
to the call of Jesus? The urgency was based upon *the
very presence of Jesus himself.* Jesus was not just
preaching the imminent coming of the Reign of God,
as for instance John was; he was himself the actual
appearance of the Reign. Where Jesus went, the
Reign of God went forth. When he spoke, it was
proclaimed. When he healed, drove out demons, or
raised the dead, these were signs of the actuality of
the Kingdom. His enemies could claim that it was
through an evil source that he did these things, but
Jesus used the very argument of fruitfulness to counter their objections and to challenge them to accept
God's activity. "But if it is by the Spirit of God that I
drive out demons, then the kingdom of God has come
upon you." (Mt 12:28)

It was therefore necessary that the hearers of
Jesus should not delay, for the Word was being

spoken, and the word had its time. The call was coming now. Jesus was present, and in his presence there was the opportunity for conversion. "We have to do the works of the one who sent me while it is day. Night is coming when no one can work. While I am in the world, I am the light of the world." (Jn 9:4-5) And so those who heard Jesus speak could not excuse themselves or afford to wait, for the time to hear God's invitation was short. If time was essential to the message of Jesus, however, it was a particular type of time.

We would be misled if we felt that Jesus was concerned for the urgency of his mission because he knew he only had about three years of earthly ministry to do everything he felt he had to do, or that somehow he knew his death would catch up to him before he would be able to get a good organization started. From this point of view, time was of no concern to Jesus at all, for he was not concerned with the calendar time of days, months, and years. Jesus was involved with another kind of time, the time we call *kairos.* This *kairos* time does not exist by the clock. Instead, it designates a particular moment, a moment of opportunity, a time of salvation. The moment of *kairos* is a moment of grace, a manifestation of God's invitation to life presented only now. The question of *kairos* is always: Will the moment be seized?

It is indeed curious that while *kairos* seems to be of utmost importance to Jesus, and plays an essential role in his preaching about conversion, we hear relatively little about it in theological writings and sermons. It is curious but not surprising, for our society has not placed a very high priority on this kind of time. Time is, of course, *very* important to us. Many of us live our lives out of our pocket calendars, our days planned months ahead of time. We rise in the morning, and begin to plan out the day that lies ahead of us. "Where has the time gone?" we think. "If I could just get more hours in the day," we say as we wolf down our microwave dinners. Even those of us who minister the Word of God do so on tightly controlled schedules. But this kind of thinking makes it very difficult to comprehend *kairos* time. Our attempts to do as many things at one time as we possibly can may be rewarded by our culture, but it places most of us at a grave disadvantage in seeking to recognize the Kingdom.

One who learns this lesson in an embarrassing manner is Martha, as recorded in Lk 10:38-42. The Christian tradition has been fond of making this incident of Mary and Martha into a reflection on prayer and work, contemplation and action. Mary, of course, in this regard has chosen the better part. This line of thought clearly reflects a bias in favor of religious life by many spiritual writers, who themselves were mostly religious, and therefore represented what we could call a "special interest group." In recent years, now that those who lead the "active life" are not seen as second-class Christians (at least in theory), there has been the temptation to refurbish Martha's tarnished reputation. All this, however, misses the obvious point of the incident. Martha, working through some resentments toward her sister, who is not helping with the preparations of hospitality, slides into an attempt to manipulate Jesus (not smart!). "Lord, do you not care that my sister has left me by myself to do the serving? Tell her to help me." The reply Jesus offers to her demonstrates this one important feature of *kairos.* "Martha, Martha, you are anxious and worried about many things. There is need of only one thing. Mary has chosen the better part and it will not be taken from her." Jesus is present, the Reign of God is being proclaimed; this is the only thing that now matters. Service, good manners, dutiful conduct, even familial love and respect, all take a relative position to the Kingdom offered at this moment. Mary seizes this moment of grace and opportunity; it cannot be denied her.

Of course, any good businessman knows that to be a success one has to seize the opportunity. And so it is perhaps with a sense of high irony that Jesus, who urges his disciples to take nothing for their journey, makes use of free enterprise as one of his favorite metaphors for explaining *kairos.* We have, for instance, the parable of the talents in Chapter 25 of Matthew's gospel, with a parallel in Luke's gospel. It is unfortunate that "talent" is so often misunderstood as an ability or skill, for that is in some way to misread the story. The parable is not primarily about what I do with my abilities, or how some people receive more gifts from God than others. A talent is a sum of money; in fact, it is a large sum of money. And the parable is primarily about making investments. The servants in question are given a golden opportunity to ride to prosperity on the coattails of a powerful benefactor. The various servants handle this opportunity differently, but the one who has the least to lose, who received only one talent, buried the money out of fear. When the master hears this, the servant, far from being praised for his caution, is reprimanded for failing to seize the opportunity (Mt 25:14-30). In *kairos* time decisive action is necessary. The disciple of the Kingdom cannot be timid or afraid. The parable does not mention what might have happened if one of the servants had lost the money, but the point of the story was never to be directed to the outcome of the investments. It was, instead, to focus on the decisive action necessary in responding to what we are presented with.

In this sense we can say that *kairos* must be responded to with spiritual initiative. The disciple must be creative with the opportunities of grace. This is presented boldly by Jesus in the parable of the dishonest steward (Lk 16:1-8), a parable that we hear with some squeamishness, since the protagonist in the story actually acts immorally. The steward, in fact, has few redeeming qualities. He has squandered his master's property and is probably guilty of more than mere mismanagement. Admittedly he is too proud to lower his station in life and is not even inclined to honest work. He comes up with a plan to embezzle money from his master through a conspiracy with his master's debtors, hoping to provide for himself in their being beholden to him. It sounds like a plot from a primetime soap opera, but in fact the master actually commends the steward. For what? There is really only one thing the steward does right, and that is, he *acts* on the moment. Perhaps he is ruthless, but there is a wisdom to this ruthlessness. Jesus goes on to comment that those who seek worldly enterprise are wiser in this regard than the disciples, the children of light, who are to be acting toward the enterprise of the Kingdom.

It is important to act on the *now* moment, the moment of *kairos,* because the opportunity may not come again. If one misses this moment, it is past. This is seen most clearly in the parable of the ten bridesmaids (Mt 25:1-13). While some commentators have sought to demonstrate that the circumstances of the parable could well have been drawn from everyday Semitic life,[6] it seems that there are at least some elements of the story that are artificially constructed. Even if it is possible that bridegrooms come at midnight, it is unlikely one would find a merchant of oil open at that hour. And even though it is hard to accept that in real everyday circumstances the bridegroom would definitively exclude from the wedding festivities those maidens who lacked the foresight to prepare for all eventualities, in the parable, by contrast, that is the focal point of the story. Bad enough everyone went to sleep, but who is prepared for the unexpected coming of the bridegroom? Those are wise who are ready to act upon the moment. One must be ready when the bridegroom comes, for the opportunity will not be repeated. The door will be locked, and those who had not been prepared to act

---

[6] William Barclay, for instance, cites a contemporary incident that is striking in its many parallels with the storyline of the parable. Barclay, William. *The Gospel of Matthew, Vol. 2.* Revised Ed. Philadelphia: Westminster Press, 1975.

will hear the chilling words, "Amen, I say to you, I do not know you." (Mt 25:12)

For Jesus, then, the primary stance of the disciple at this *now* moment is one of vigilance. The disciple must always be awake and alert for the coming of the Reign at any time. "Therefore, stay awake! For you do not know on which day your Lord will come. Be sure of this: if the master of the house had known the hour of night when the thief was coming, he would have stayed awake and not let his house be broken into. So too, you also must be prepared, for at an hour you do not expect, the Son of Man will come." (Mt 24:42-44) In this passage the attitudes of preparedness and alertness have been brought together. While the Son of Man's coming will usher in the end time, there can be no delay in assuming those attitudes now. The alertness for *kairos* must be constant.

> Beware that your hearts do not become drowsy from carousing and drunkenness and the anxieties of daily life, and that day catch you by surprise like a trap. For that day will assault everyone who lives on the face of the earth. Be vigilant at all times and pray that you have the strength to escape the tribulations that are imminent and to stand before the Son of Man. (Lk 21:34-36)

This sense of vigilance that Jesus speaks of is the stance of "consciousness" used in some of the writings on the Enneagram. It is that awareness of the present moment and an openness to receive the grace offered within it. The disciple must be alert and awake, not drowsy. Jesus tells us, "Gird your loins and light your lamps and be like servants who await their master's return from a wedding, ready to open immediately when he comes and knocks." Then Jesus goes on to offer a beatitude for the vigilant disciple. "Blessed are those servants whom the master finds vigilant on his arrival. Amen, I say to you, he will gird himself, have them recline at table, and proceed to wait on them." (Lk 12:35-37) The blessing Jesus offers the vigilant servant is a reversal of what is expected. As a guest invited to a banquet, the servant will be honored, a sign, not of slavery, but of friendship (Jn 15:15-16).

THE WISE AND THE FOOLISH

Who is the disciple now ready to hear the Good News given in this *kairos* moment? We have seen that it is someone who must be awake to this present moment, someone who is vigilant and prepared to meet with openness the inbreaking of every invitation of grace. This disciple of the Lord would truly be a special kind of person. It would no doubt require someone who had a great sense of trust in God. This disciple would also be one who had experienced within that penetrating call to conversion. We could also expect this person to be someone possessing a special kind of discernment, a special kind of wisdom.

When we think of the word "wisdom" in scripture, the first thing that comes to mind is probably that general grouping of works in the Old Testament that is known as the wisdom literature. The books of Proverbs, and Wisdom, and so forth, represent an important segment of Hebrew literature that was generally quite different from the Torah and the prophetic writings. In many ways the wisdom literature of the Old Testament was more cosmopolitan than the other major types of writings. It developed out of and was highly influenced by similar kinds of literature in the wider Semitic world around Israel. Wisdom literature was not concerned so much with kings and treaties, not with the temple and the priesthood. It was meant as a down-to-earth, everyday, practical aid in life, how to live in astute reverence for God.

Wisdom literature, like the other forms of Old Testament writings, had a great impact on the New Testament. In the gospel of John, for instance, we can reflect on some basic concepts from wisdom literature that have greatly influenced the structure of John's understanding of Jesus. We find, for instance, particularly in the prologue of the gospel, Jesus portrayed as the pre-existent Word, the *Logos*, spoken of in thought patterns strikingly similar to those that that personify Wisdom, *hokmah*, in Wisdom 7 and Proverbs 8. John's portrayal of Jesus as the "light of the world" and the "bread come down from heaven" are reflected in wisdom literature, as, for instance, in Wisdom 16-18.

But there is another kind of wisdom found in the gospels. It is not a wisdom that others apply to Jesus, but instead is a wisdom that Jesus encourages others to seek. We hear of this wisdom in the gospels of Matthew and Luke. We have already met this call to be wise in our overview of the teaching of Jesus on the Reign of God and on conversion, because it is closely linked to the call to be vigilant in seeking the inbreaking of God in *kairos*. Jesus speaks of the need for his disciples to be wise, and he warns them against a contrary tendency, that is, the foolish action of one who is not pursuing the path of discipleship.

When Jesus speaks of this kind of wisdom in the gospels, the Greek word used is the adjective *phronimos* and other related grammatical structures. In one sense it simply means being wise or intelligent. It has this connotation, for instance, when used by Paul in First Corinthians (10:15), but in the gospels it means much more. When Jesus speaks of being *phronimos*, he is urging the disciple to a wisdom that is at once both prudent and clever. The disciple who possesses such wisdom is one who is mindful of the truest interests of self.

This wisdom is the wisdom of the five bridesmaids in Matthew 25 who were prepared for the bridegroom's coming. It is the one redeeming quality possessed by the ruthless steward in Luke 16, commended by his master for his ability to "act wisely" (vs. 8). The wise one, therefore, possesses the qualities that enable her or him to take advantage of *kairos*. She is determined and alert, ready to act on what the moment requires. The wise one knows what is truly in the best interests of the self, and has taken appropriate measures to insure his acceptance of the Kingdom. Above all, then, the wise one is a disciple, in the most authentic sense of the word. While having the innocence of a dove, still the disciple is *phronimos* as a serpent (Mt 10:16). "Who, then, is the faithful and wise servant, whom the master has put in charge of his household to distribute to them their food at the proper time? Blessed is that servant whom the master on his arrival finds doing so. Amen, I say to you, he will put this one in charge of all his property." (Mt 24:45-47) This beatitude is also paralleled in Lk 12:42-44.

Opposite one who is wise, however, stands one whose actions are foolish, *mōros.* This does not simply mean uneducated, or even silly. The fool is one whose actions are ill-advised in response to the Kingdom, one who is unprepared, asleep, and obtuse in regard to the invitation of grace. The contrast between the wise and the foolish has a long tradition in Semitic wisdom literature. It is, for instance, a common structure in the wisdom writings of the Old Testament. For example, we see in Sir 21:11-28 the contrasting behavior between the wise one and the fool. The wise one's "knowledge wells up in a flood, and counsel, like a living spring; a fool's mind is like a broken jar -- no knowledge at all can it hold." (vs. 13-14) In Proverbs 9 we see the offering of two banquets, one hosted by Wisdom, who has prepared a sumptuous feast for all who seek her ways of understanding. The other meal is offered by Folly, stolen water and ill-gotten bread for any who would come her way.

With this passage, however, we begin to get a hint of a deeper issue beneath the wise and the foolish. At issue is not simply the wise one's grasp of knowledge or understanding. Foolishness is not the concoction of harebrained schemes. The real issue of true wisdom is conversion. Wisdom is found by those who forsake the path of wickedness, and turn their steps to ways of righteousness. The literature is quick to point out that wisdom has its origins in the reverence or fear of God. The author of Sirach says, "The beginning of wisdom is fear of the Lord, which is formed with the faithful in the womb. With the devoted was she created from of old, and with their children her beneficence abides. Fullness of wisdom is fear of the Lord; she inebriates all with her fruits." (Sir 1:12-14)[7] This fear of the Lord arises from a profound sense of awe before the Creator, a knowing of God and a desire to do God's will.

In a similar way, foolishness is directly equated with wickedness. The fool is the one who lives in sin and believes that there will not be an accounting. The psalmist cries out, "How great are your works, O Lord! How very deep are your thoughts! A senseless man knows not, nor does a fool understand this. Though the wicked flourish like grass and all evildoers thrive, they are destined for eternal destruction; while you, O Lord, are the Most High forever." (Ps 92:6-9) The fool, who has no respect or fear of God, who has not observed the wisdom of virtuous living, turns to wrong-doing, believing it to be advantageous. "The fool says in the heart, 'There is no God.' Such are corrupt; they do abominable deeds; there is not one who does good. The Lord looks down from heaven upon the children of humankind, to see if there be one who is wise and seeks God." (Ps 14:1-2)

---

[7]   See also: Job 28:28; Ps 111:10; Prov 1:7; Sir 19:17

The wisdom movement of the Near East, passed on as it was through the writings of scribes and the learned ones of court, had a significant influence. The wisdom literature of Israel, which was the most intact and ultimately the most influential, had a great impact, not only on the New Testament, but also on the Talmud and other Near Eastern literature. The literature of Sufism, for instance, resounds with echoes of the wise and the foolish. The true Sufi, the one who knows the path of knowledge, seeks to follow that path to the Real. In contrast, the idiot has mindlessly gone astray, losing the way of the path while believing he or she is still in pursuit of knowledge.

While the teachings of Jesus were also influenced by the wisdom language of the wise and the foolish, the use that Jesus makes of them is totally in line with his preaching of the Reign and conversion. While the one who is truly wise seizes the moment of conversion offered in the words of Jesus, the fool misses it.

> Everyone who listens to these words of mine and acts on them will be like a wise man who built his house on rock. The rains fell, the floods came, and the winds blew and buffeted the house. But it did not collapse; it had been set solidly on rock. And everyone who listens to these words of mine but does not act on them will be like a fool who built his house on sand. The rain fell, the floods came, and the winds blew and buffeted the house. And it col-

lapsed and was completely ruined. (Mt 7:24-27)

The fool's collapse is a theme that Jesus focuses on. Not only is the fool ill-prepared, as with the foolish bridesmaids, but the preparations they do make are to no avail, and in fact are counter-productive. Jesus rebukes the rich fool, who wants to build bigger barns on the night that his life will be demanded (Lk 12:16-21). Conversion is a present experience, and cannot be reached by living in the future. Jesus also denounces the scribes and Pharisees as blind fools (Mt 23:17), not because they do not have knowledge, but because of their obstinancy and self-deception. This is echoed in the gospel of John (Jn 9:39-41) where their blindness is in their determination to claim to see.

By way of conclusion on Jesus' teaching on the wise, my own fascination with difficult scripture passages takes me back to our friend, the ruthless but *phronimos* steward (Lk 16:1-8). He does only one thing right, and is duly praised for it by Jesus. He seizes the moment of *kairos*. This passage itself presents enough difficulty to preachers that I cannot help but relate it to two even more difficult parallel passages in Matthew and Luke. These are the passages about taking the Kingdom by violence (Mt 11:12 and Lk 16:16). It seems likely that even the evangelists did not know what to do with the passage, which probably accounts for the minor variations in the parallels. I cannot say that I have ever been fully satisfied with commentaries I have read on the passages, most of which acknowledge the difficulty, but offer little by way of solution. My own comments are admittedly only speculative. Is there a hint of an understanding of the passages through the action of the ruthless steward? Is Jesus suggesting that to seize the moment of *kairos* is to capture the Kingdom, to carry it away as booty, as the verb in the passages suggests? If this is the case, then the disciple is the one who must act with ruthless initiative, breaching the walls of personal resistance and snatching the Reign from one's own spiritual languor. It has caused me to speculate that there is perhaps a Gospel call to *live the spiritual life ruthlessly*. Is the truly spiritual woman or man one who is relentless in self-honesty, persistent in seeking conversion, and resolute in the efforts to bear fruit worthy of the Reign of God at the cost of all one holds dear? Is the hidden treasure worth such a high price? But before buying into the ruthless living of the spiritual life, I would caution the reader to examine one more dimension of the teachings of Jesus, the call to compassionate living.

HEARTFELT COMPASSION

There is a saying about "traditional" Catholic asceticism, and that is that it has to feel bad to be good. Most Catholics I know laugh at this, because we know that while it is a gross misstatement of something worth taking seriously, it is indeed reminiscent of how many of us were brought up. There was, to be sure, a feeling we received in the pre-Vatican II Church that if it was something I wanted or desired, it was probably not what God wanted. Likewise, the will of God was undoubtedly the toughest thing going, probably not something I would choose of my own accord. Unhappily, many old attitudes die hard, and it is not difficult to find a fair amount of this ascetical attitude still around.

I mention this because I can imagine some would-be ascetics licking their mortified chops over the prospect of living the spiritual life "ruthlessly." So I need to present an important statement at the very outset. The disciple, it seems to me, must be "ruthless" in pursuing the Reign of God, but *always* with compassion. I believe I am on solid ground in saying this, because I feel it is in keeping with the picture that all the gospels consistently paint of Jesus, both in what he says and in what he does. I can think of no more universally true statement than to say that Jesus always manifested the compassionate love of God.

There is, of course, a difference between compassion and enabling, which many in our contemporary society are only slowly and painfully learning. I do not mean to imply, therefore, that Jesus was an enabler, that he went around allowing people to continue in patterns of destructive behavior. We remember, for instance, how he responded to Martha. He spoke the truth to her about her anxieties and concerns, not reinforcing her manipulations, but then also encouraged her to go beyond her limited thinking and pursue the *one thing* offered. Perhaps the most compassionate thing that Jesus offers Martha, and each of us as well, is the opportunity to seek discipleship.

In speaking about discipleship and compassion, however, there is one small problem we must first deal with. The disciple, we have come to believe from deal with. The disciple, we have come to believe from scripture, is called to perfection. "So be perfect, just as your heavenly Father is perfect." (Mt 5:48) Doesn't this mean that anyone who wants to be a disciple has to begin weeding out all those flaws and blemishes that permeate human existence? Aren't we to sift through our thoughts, emotions, and behaviors, seeking to eradicate vices, making a constant effort toward improvement? Maybe I can be compassionate toward others (and, of course, I *should* do that perfectly!), but how does scripture allow me to be compassionate with myself? As I say, we have a small problem when we deal with compassion. Yet it is important to realize that it is *our* problem, and not scripture's. The Gospel calls us to be perfect *and* compassionate (even to ourselves). In fact, there is good reason to believe that if I cannot be compassionate toward myself, I stand little chance of truly having compassion for a sister or brother.

What, then, is this perfection we are authentically called to pursue, even while demonstrating self-compassion? Once more we go to the Greek word, hoping it can help us with a deeper understanding. The word used by Matthew is the word *teleios*, which means: brought to its end, wanting nothing necessary for its completeness, finished, and therefore, by extension, perfect. Applied to humans it often means full-grown or mature. It is worth noting what it does not mean. It does not, in itself, carry the sense of flawless behavior. It has come to mean this because of how *we* understand perfection. We think of perfection linearly, a straight line of permanent improvement that will lead us to where we are "supposed to be," that is, in the "state" of flawlessness. David L. Miller believes, on the contrary, that in their origins *teleios* and its cognates were really developed out of a language structure that referred to circular things. The word *telos*, from which *teleios* is derived, means an end or termination, but is used often in a more ancient Greek in the context of various kinds of wrappings, such as a wedding band, a champion's crown, city walls, or even a death shroud.[8] In this sense, we can see the "end" in question as possessing the connotation of inclusion or of destiny.

This understanding of *teleios* can help us imagine perfection out of *our* human experience, just as the Church Fathers and the medieval scholastics imagined it out of their experience of Greek philosophy. We can understand perfection as the completion of a destiny, the destiny we were called to in the Reign of God. Perfection is the fulfillment of our discipleship, the discovery of our truest nature in the likeness of God, the experience of our wholeness and full maturity in Christ. Is this definition any further from the intention of Jesus than the perfection of the scholastics? I would tend to think the opposite. Jesus is not

---

[8] Miller pursues this line of thought in his treatment of perfection, going on to suggest that the "end" of perfection is endless, and that we must provide ways of restructuring our theology of Christ in order to allow the imagining of our failures, our *im*perfections. Miller, David L. *Christs: Meditations on Archetypal Images in Christian Theology.* New York: The Seabury Press, 1981. pp. 3-26.

portrayed as demanding flawless behavior of people,[9] and in fact criticizes the Pharisees, who seem to be doing just that. Instead, Jesus is intent upon conveying the unlimited love of God, first revealed in the Covenant, and most clearly expressed in compassion. We should not be surprised, then, when we look at Luke's parallel of Matthew 5:48, to discover that we are called, not to be as perfect as God is, but to be as compassionate as God is (Lk 6:36). Jesus, in Luke's gospel, then goes on to spell out exactly what this means. Stop judging! Stop condemning! Instead, begin forgiving, and forgiveness will be given in turn (vs. 37). Then Jesus offers a promise that is certainly in line with our revised definition of perfection. "Give and gifts will be given to you; a good measure, packed together, shaken down, and overflowing, will be poured into your lap. For the measure with which you measure will in return be measured out to you." (Lk 6:38)

If we are to be as compassionate as God, then certainly the gospels offer no end of examples for us in the actions and words of Jesus. The ministry of Jesus is one of compassion. The Reign of God is proclaimed in an atmosphere of mercy. The signs and

---

[9] There are, of course, passages such as Mt 5:29-30, where Jesus urges a person to tear out an eye or cut off a hand if it is a cause of sin. It is doubtful, however, that this was ever meant to be more than a metaphor for the "ruthless" pursuit of conversion. At least the Christian tradition has judged it prudent to interpret it so.

works of power performed by Jesus are works that are born out of compassion, and in turn they bear witness that the Reign of God is present. Jesus has compassion for the poor, for they are powerless and have no one to protect them. He shows mercy to those who are hungry, for they have been deprived of their needs. He has compassion for those who are in sorrow, and seek to understand their loss and grief. And he grants mercy to those who have known exclusion, especially due to their preaching of the Gospel. He offers a blessing upon them, and a great reward in the Kingdom. (Lk 6:20-23)

Often in the gospels, when Jesus acts with compassion or speaks about compassion it is linked with the word for entrails or bowels. This is usually translated as something similar to "having heartfelt compassion" or "moved to pity." At the time of Jesus the entrails were considered the seat of intense emotions, such as love or hate. We hear, then, of Jesus looking out over the crowd that has followed him, overcome with troubles, exhausted, harassed, abandoned, and he is "moved with compassion." (Mt 9:36) While we today do not often connect emotion with the entrails, we do have a related expression called a "gut reaction." We know when we have a gut reaction; it cannot escape our attention. We spontaneously respond with passion, or lash out in anger. For Jesus compassion is a gut reaction. There is no hesitation, no deliberation, only the necessary action of mercy. That is how Jesus is; that is how God is. And unmistakably that is how Jesus calls the disciple to be.

Jesus understands his own ministry of compassion as manifested in his role as servant. In a similar manner, the attitude of his disciples is to be that of servants. This is not fully appreciated by the Twelve, who have, as Peter points out to Jesus, left all to follow him (Lk 18:28). They argue about who is the greatest. James and John get in their bids for the prize places. Jesus tells them:

> You know that those who are recognized as rulers over the Gentiles lord it over them, and their great ones make their authority over them felt. But it shall not be so among you. Rather, whoever wishes to be great among you will be your servant; whoever wishes to be first among you will be the slave of all. For the Son of Man did not come to be served but to serve and to give his life as a ransom for many. (Mk 10:42-45)

In John's gospel, at the Last Supper, Jesus washes the feet of the disciples (Jn 13:1-17). John uses language that is clearly metaphoric of the Lord's impending death and resurrection (vs. 4 and 12). This washing of feet, Jesus tells them, is meant as an example to them. "If I, therefore, the master and teacher, have washed your feet, you ought to wash one another's feet. I have given you a model to follow, so that as I have done for you, you should also do." (vs. 14-15)

The compassion to which Jesus calls his disciples begins with each one's own pursuit of the Reign of

God. In moving through conversion toward that perfection of wholeness, the disciple must have compassion for himself or herself. We are to love others as we love ourselves (Mk 12:31); how then can we hope to be true servants for one another if we cannot show respect and compassion for ourselves? Compassion directed toward the self is frequently demonstrated in the effort of building up within oneself dignity and self-esteem. In this regard, we can look at the cure of the crippled woman recorded in Lk 13:10-17.

Jesus is teaching in the synagogue on the Sabbath, and he sees a woman, crippled by a spirit for eighteen years. The gospel says that she was bent over, completely incapable of lifting herself up. It is worth noting that the word used here can have both a physical and a psychological sense. Later in the gospel we see the same word used to encourage those who await their redemption by the Son of Man; they are to stand erect and lift their heads (Lk 21:28). Jesus cures the woman, and she stands up straight. However, the synagogue leader is intensely angry, no doubt at Jesus, but he directs his anger at the woman for being cured on the Sabbath. There is the clear indication that the man feels somehow threatened by this new development, although he never acknowledges it. This causes Jesus to retort with a scathing analogy.

> The Lord said to him in reply, "Hypocrites! Does not each one of you on the sabbath untie his ox or his ass from the manger and lead it out for watering? This daughter of

Abraham, whom Satan has bound for eighteen years now, ought she not to have been set free on the sabbath day from this bondage?" When he said this, all his adversaries were humiliated; and the whole crowd rejoiced at all the splendid deeds done by him. (vs.15-17)

The sacredness of the Sabbath is protected by the Law, and the Law in turn is to manifest the Covenant, and yet exceptions are commonly made in regard to the care of beasts of burden. How can an exception be denied to this daughter of the Covenant, whom the Law is meant to protect? There is a clue in the vehemence of Jesus' response that suggests part of the nature of the woman's trouble. Jesus sees the oppressive structure of this patriarchal social order as at least partially responsible for keeping her bent over, unable to stand upright, to view herself as righteous under the Covenant. In healing her Jesus also calls her to a new "life stance," and to a new way of experiencing herself.

The same attitude that Jesus demonstrates in this healing story is repeated again and again in his presence to the sinners and the outcasts he meets in his preaching. While he calls them to conversion, he also bestows upon them a new sense of self-esteem through the very experience of dignity they receive from him. The compassion Jesus shows toward others is largely directed toward their establishing a greater sense of worth within themselves. We hear, for instance, the words Jesus speaks to the Pharisees when they criticize his dining with sinners. "Those who are not well do not need a physician, but the sick do. Go and learn the meaning of the words, 'I desire mercy, not sacrifice.' I did not come to call the righteous but sinners." (Mt 9:12-13) There is a compassion that goes beyond the form of religion; the one who has strayed is in need of healing, not condemnation.

When a person has come to a place of self-compassion, there is no longer the insatiable need to protect oneself, one's ego.[10] I can let go of my need to explain myself and seek more to understand the other. The ability to get beyond myself, my needs, my desires, my image, my status, is the secret of Gospel compassion. It is the stance taken by the Good Samaritan (Lk 10:29-37) in the parable we probably most identify with Jesus' teaching on compassion. The priest and Levite, those bound by the Law to offer aid and hospitality, pass the one who has fallen victim to

---

[10] "Ego" is a problematic word in contemporary psychological writing, because it means different things to different people. Often the ego is spoken of positively, as the result of a healthy process of maturation. We hear, for instance, some writers speak of "ego strength." Others understand the word in a more negative fashion. In this sense, ego stands counterpoint to the self, the false self to the true self. It is this sense of the word that I seek to consistently use throughout this book. I do caution the reader, however, to be aware of the two uses, and in general, to note how the limitations of our language can cause confusion of experiences.

robbers either because of the distasteful nature of the task or because of its inconvenience. The Samaritan, who has nothing personal to gain from helping, is the one who is "moved with compassion." (vs. 33) He is the one capable of getting outside of himself, and offering aid to a fellow human being.

The opposite of compassion, therefore, we could call self-interest. Here we once more meet Jesus, the storyteller, and his liking for paradox. On one hand, Jesus praises the dishonest steward of Luke 16 for his wise sense of self-interest. It is, of course, an interest directed toward the true self and the pursuit of the Reign. There is, however, another kind of self-interest, the interests of ego, of the self lost in the self. With this self-interest I have no room for compassion, in fact, I have no room for anything. My whole being is consumed with self-enlargement and self-protection.

Jesus, the storyteller, illustrates this other type of self-interest in the parable of the unforgiving servant (Mt 18:23-35). The king, in the story, has a servant brought to him who owes him something equivalent to the national debt. At the man's pleading, the king is "moved with compassion," (vs. 27) and writes off the entire debt. But the servant immediately goes outside and meets another servant who basically owes him pocket change. Demanding that he be paid, the first servant is not content with the promise to make good on the loan, but throws the second servant into prison. In the unforgiving servant's inability to get beyond his own self-interest, he has lost all sight of proportions. Quite often our perspective on reality is one of the first casualties of self-centeredness.

On the other hand, the story also demonstrates that one of the first fruits of compassion is forgiveness. In a real sense, forgiveness is the measure of compassion. That is why compassion can never be solely directed to the distant masses. It will always involve, sooner or later, its demonstration in the here and now with those I am called to interact with. The context of the parable of the unforgiving servant is forgiveness, and not compassion per se. It is introduced by Jesus' statement on the "perfection" of forgiveness, which is not "seven times but seventy-seven times." (Mt 18:22) Forgiveness, as with compassion, is to be understood as being unlimited.

The parable of the forgiving father (Lk 15:11-32) shows once more the connection between forgiveness, compassion, and love. The compassion the father has for his wayward son, and the forgiveness he is anxious to bestow, are the result of his unwavering love for him. Forgiveness is seen in the parable, and throughout the ministry of Jesus, as the manifestation of love. God's love of humanity is boundless. It does not keep score; it does not show favorites. Like the father in the parable, God continues to seek every opportunity to bestow love on humanity.

While Jesus reveals to us a God who is ready to forgive us unconditionally, and to do so innumerable times, it is also clear that Jesus most desires that the love upon which forgiveness and compassion are based be mutual. Jesus asks his disciples to show in return the love that's appropriate for what they have been given. This exchange of love, the great commandment of the Covenant, in turn will bring about the fruitfulness of the Reign of God. This mutual exchange of love is demonstrated in the compassion shown to all God's children. The judgment we will receive is that of our own actions of love and forgiveness, or conversely of our inaction. What we have done to the least of our brothers and sisters is the litmus test of our own response to the invitation to the Kingdom (Mt 25:31-46).

TWO

THE CHRISTIAN EXPERIENCE

THE STORY

The kingdom of heaven may be likened to a man who sowed good seed in his field, but then, strangely, he and all his household went to sleep. They were sure that the seed would grow of its own accord. But an enemy sowed weeds all through the wheat, and disappeared. As the crop grew and began to bear fruit, it was discovered that something else was growing in the field. The householder recognized it as a weed, but the plants were still small and it was hard to distinguish one from another.

There were also slaves in the household, who possessed the mentality so frequently associated with slaves: they felt themselves in bondage. They had their own opinion of the weeds. At first they questioned whether good seed had been sown in the field to begin with. Then, of course, they felt the best thing to do would be to go into the field and pull up everything that looked like it might be a weed. The householder mysteriously rejected this idea, and directed that everything be allowed to grow together.

The master of the household also had other fields with other crops. It was discovered that there were weeds in these fields as well. With each discovery, the slaves again counseled to eradicate the weeds, but each time the master held them back. Of course, they felt this was one more proof of their slavery. They began to question the householder, and even wondered if he might not actually be the enemy. After all, he apparently wanted the weeds to remain. But slowly the master's reasoning came to light. As each crop matured and ripened, its fruit was openly discernible. Now it was time for the harvest, and it was clear what was fruitful and what wasn't. It was also discovered that often what was initially thought to be a weed was, in fact, not a weed at all, but simply a different kind of plant. Often these plants also produced fruit, some very exotic and valuable, but of different sorts than what was expected. When the harvesters went out (slaves no longer, for there can be no true slaves at harvest time) they found fruit in abundance, each in its own proper growing season. What needed to be discarded was thrown out and burned, but the householder was amazed. This season had been his most fruitful one of all.   (Based on Mt 13:24-30)

THE ROOTS OF CHRISTIANITY

It is easy to take our own experiences as normative -- to presume, for instance, that our culture is the correct culture, that our ethnic group has the true perspective, that our family did things the proper way -- and it is only ignorance that would make anyone want to be different. Until our experiences teach us differently, we tend to hold as true our unique perspective on reality. This is very much the case with our religious experience as well. If we are middle-class American Christians, we might tend to think of Christianity as something essential to being middle-class and American. Some time ago I saw a picture of the Last Supper with all the apostles kneeling at a communion rail and Jesus distributing little white wafers to them on their tongues. This image adequately spoofs the very point.

So it is necessary to take some time to remind ourselves that Christianity began in a Semitic world 2000 years ago. It was a world very different from our own. It was not a world of high technology and modern conveniences. It was not a religion born on a Madison Avenue drawing board, or even in a diocesan committee meeting. Christianity was born in the desert. It was born out of the experience of Israel, a religion that emerged from the desert. The desert was where John the Baptist preached, where Jesus went to meet the realities of life and there to be tempted. The first generations of Christians were people familiar with the desert, who understood its harshness and knew the demands it placed on survival. The world that Christianity first experienced, the world of first-century Judaism, was one that offered little comfort. The desert created cultures that did not take life for granted. In many ways, it is still harsh and unyielding, even in our present day.

The world first experienced by the early Christians was a concrete world; it did not lend itself to abstractions and subtleties. There was the sky and the sun, the rocks and the parched earth. There was the need for food and water; there was the need for shelter from the elements. It was a world that dealt better with facts than with theories, with physical realities than with ideas. The language structure that desert life created was concrete as well. It emphasized image over concept, things seen and named rather than the fruit of speculative thought. The Greeks had their philosophers; but Semites experienced the world too immediately to venture far into metaphysics.

The Semitic world experienced humankind concretely as well. At first, survival was a matter of the family, the clan, or the tribe. The individual was of little account until about the time of the Exile. Even after that, there were strong family and group bonds that cannot be underestimated, and that show themselves even in today's world arena. The human person in the Semitic mind was whole and undivided. The individual was not a body/soul dichotomy in the Aristotelian sense, nor a manifestation of a Platonic ideal. The person was understood to be enfleshed spirit. Many words were used for describing the person, all of them born out of the lived experience.

> The same use of bodily parts for inner qualities is found in biblical passages that describe the person as living "flesh" or "spirit," or declare that someone's "heart" planned evil or "kidneys" rejoiced. Humans are made up of flesh (*basar*), spirit (*ruah*), heart (*leb*) and soul (*nepesh*). All of these words have many different meanings, and each passage must be treated separately to understand what the authors mean to say about a person.[1]

---

[1] Boadt, Lawrence. *Reading the Old Testament.* p. 247.

As the Semitic world of early Christianity understood life and the person in stark and concrete ways, so sin was expressed concretely as well. The Jewish culture, out of which the Christian experience was born, understood human sinfulness as rebellion (Dt 9:24). This was modeled in Scripture after Israel's desert grumbling. In the books of Exodus and Numbers the people continuously complain of their treatment at the hands of Moses (who is only *God's* instrument). They seek to abort the process of their liberation, and they plunge into what is the most serious form of sin in the Old Testament -- idolatry (Ex 32:1-6; Num 14:2-4).

Within the religious culture of Israel, sin could always be seen in some way as a rebellion against God, and a seeking of some other "god." In the prophetic literature this often took the form of power-seeking, particularly in the form of political alliances. The prophets also decried the sin of social injustice, which put one's own desires before the good of others. Sin was a seeking of one's own way at the expense of the brother or sister. Long before Jesus referred to those around him as an evil generation, God had complained to Moses about this "stiff-necked" people who so determinedly sought their own will (Ex 32:9).

As sin was imaged in concrete terms, so was conversion. As stated earlier, the most common word used in the Old Testament to express the action of conversion is *sûb*. It does not have the subtle interior connotations of *metanoeō*, but is much richer in imagery. It suggests a change of direction, a turning back to a former place, just what needed to be done when one's own aimless wanderings had led one too far into the cruelty of desert sun and heat. In the Jewish experience of salvation, the return that was necessary was to the Covenant, the love relationship with God.

While the Covenant relationship was seen primarily as that of Sinai, the image of covenant became a favorite theological expression of God's care for the people. God was seen as continuously reestablishing and reaffirming love for Israel. A covenant had been established with Abraham, and later during the monarchy a covenant was made with David. Jeremiah spoke of a new covenant, one that would be written upon the hearts of all Israel (Jer 31:31-34).

All these covenants (which were really only one) were initiated by God. It was God who had sought out Israel in the desert, God who had elected to love Israel, sometimes for no apparent reason. While God's ways were perhaps mysterious, in faith there could be no doubt -- Israel was a *chosen* people. God had freely decided to bestow love upon this people. Earlier in Israel's history this election had been understood in light of the belief that Yahweh was the God of Israel in contrast to the other nations. The peoples beyond Israel had other gods, or at least believed they did, but Israel had been found by the true God. The other gods were as nothing, Yahweh was the only real God, and Israel was God's *special possession* (Ex 19:5).

Israel's belief in its own election had a profound effect upon the development of the nation's identity. Were they not God's chosen, God's people? And what did this say about their relationship with the other nations, the Gentiles? These peoples, after all, continued to cling to their mistaken beliefs. As a theology of monotheism became more completely established in Israel, a wider separation took hold. The other nations were seen as unclean, and therefore to be avoided. While the prophets cautioned Israel not to assume that it was anything the people had done that had brought about their election, still a mentality of isolation and cultural superiority took hold in many ways.

The Covenant, of course, was seen as one of love, love breaking into the starkness of desert life. It was love that had motivated God to act for the people's liberation. "For love of your fathers he chose their descendants and personally led you out of Egypt by his great power, driving out of your way nations greater and mightier than you, so as to bring you in and to make their land your heritage, as it is today." (Dt 4:37-38). And it was love that caused God to forgive so often the flagrant sins of Israel.

> When Israel was a child I loved him, out of Egypt I called my son. The more I called them, the farther they went from me, sacrificing to the Baals and burning incense to idols. Yet it was I who taught Ephraim to walk, who took them in my arms; I drew them with human cords, with bands of love; I fostered them like one who raises an infant to his cheeks; yet, though I stooped to feed my child, they did not know that I was their healer. (Hos 11:1-4)

Israel had a God of mercy. This couldn't be denied, for forgiveness was bestowed upon them again and again. But this God of mercy was also understood through the life experiences that were in keeping with their surroundings, the harshness of the desert. So God was not just a God of tenderness, but also a jealous God, one whose wrath flared up in the face of idolatry; a warrior God, the Lord of armies, one who demonstrated power in the face of an enemy; the God of the mountain, *el Shaddai*, a mysterious God one approached only with awe and fear.

We have seen how the Covenant was mediated by the Law, the way in which the Covenant was made direct, practical, and concrete. The Law was seen to be the manifestation of the Covenant. For the believing Jew it was the measure of one's righteousness, at least in the cultural and juridical sense. One who kept the Law lived in the awareness of what God expected. It attempted to explain and detail all the dimensions of individual and communal faith.

The Law, however, was also what separated Israel from the other peoples, the Gentiles. As they did not have the true God, and were not a part of the Covenant, so they were apart from the Law. As the Law had developed, it had come to *identify* Israel, to give form to its very existence. Before the Exile, Israel had been a nation, but with the Babylonian captivity any true sense of itself as a political entity was shattered. Israel was redeemed from its exile only by being cast into a Persian world, one benign enough to allow the rebuilding of the Temple. Then it found itself in the midst of a Greek world, one much less inclined to try to understand its eccentricities. Finally, laid upon this was the Roman government, so secular in its makeup it cared little about such oddities as this strange Jewish religion. Feeling themselves surrounded by a hostile cultural and religious climate, without a political reality of their own to fall back on, the Jewish people found in the Law the stabilizing element they so needed. The Law provided the religious, cultural, and social fabric that allowed for their continued survival as a people.

The Jews of Jesus' time colored their self-imposed social isolation with an air of disdain. They had to maintain their separation from Gentile culture for the sake of ritual purity; anything non-Jewish was potentially unclean. Of course, despite the numerous stipulations of the Law, the purity of the Judaic culture was something of a fiction. Being so long surrounded by people of varying backgrounds and cultures, there could not help but be an abundance of subtle and not-so-subtle influences that had crept into the daily lives of the people. Moreover, many Jews in the Diaspora were spread throughout the Greco-Roman world. They had their own cultural tendencies, their own linguistic focus, their own metropolitan outlook that further separated them from their own people.

Even religious belief had been infiltrated. During the time of the Exile many elements of Zoroastrianism, the predominant religion of Persia, had made their way into Judaism. The belief in a hierarchy of archangels, angels, and demons, the acceptance of the evil principle of the *Shaitin* (Satan), and the emphasis on a future life and individual judgment became commonly held tenets of faith. Many of the works of Scripture were greatly influenced by them. They were part of the understanding of Jesus, and they became accepted aspects of the new Christian belief.

My purpose in presenting this overview of the social and religious background that surrounded Jesus and the early Christian community is twofold. First, it helps us realize that the Christian experience, in which an understanding of conversion was a significant part, was not without its historical context. Second, I want to emphasize that at least on the surface, the first followers of Jesus emerged from a climate of cultural separation, one that to a great extent held anything foreign as suspicious, unclean, and probably unsaved. This is necessary in order to get a proper perspective on the extent to which the Christian community chose to depart from this stance.

THE SHATTERING OF INSULARITY

In reading the gospels it is not always clear how to distinguish the sayings and actions of Jesus from the transmission of them through the lived experience of the faith community, which shared its remembrances of them in light of its present circumstances. While many scholars of this century have sought the "historical Jesus," meaning a view of Jesus from a perspective prior to the Resurrection and the belief of the faith community, it is unlikely that such a view can be definitively constructed from the gospel accounts, the very existence of which depends upon the experience of Resurrection faith. Still, in many ways there is a consistency in these four portraits of Jesus that enables us to speak with some certainty about the kind of person Jesus was.

It is clear, for instance, that in his earthly ministry, despite having been raised in the cultural separation of Judaism, Jesus saw beyond the limiting social boundaries of the Law. He freely associated with those identified as sinners, with prostitutes and with those Roman collaborators who collected taxes; he did not shun the ritually unclean. The gospels show Jesus reaching out to Gentiles. He heals the centurion's servant (Mt 8:5-13), and carries on a lively exchange with the Samaritan woman (John 4:4-26). There is even some indication that experiences within his ministry might have helped expand his appreciation for those beyond the Law's reach; for instance, in the case of the Syrophonecian woman (Mk 7:24-30).

We could expect, then, that this new faith community, imbued as it was with its belief in the Risen Jesus, would not long be contained within the Law's social boundaries. The earliest Christians, however, tried to remain faithful Jews. Jesus was, after all, the Messiah, the one for whom they had been waiting. There was no reason, therefore, to believe that faith in Jesus in any way abrogated their belief in Judaism. The Acts of the Apostles portray the early community as continuing to fulfill its Jewish piety, going to the temple (Acts 2:46) and continuing to meet in synagogues with other Jews who did not share their belief in Jesus, sometimes debating the differences in their theological perspective, as in the cases of Stephen and Paul.

The earliest hint of a dispute within the community was more a Jewish problem than a Christian one.

There were tensions between a Hellenist element, which spoke Greek, and the Aramaic-speaking portion of the Jerusalem community, to which the Twelve and presumably the majority of members belonged (Acts 6:1-7). The dispute resulted in the appointment of deacons, among them leaders of the Hellenist party. While this tension more than likely was paralleled in the wider Jewish community, the solution that the early Church sought had the effect of placing in leadership roles several individuals whose perspective was open to the wider world. Still, much of the early Church remained staunchly traditional in their world view. James, who emerged as head of the Jerusalem community, seems to have been a powerful figure who no doubt represented a large portion of the early membership.

Following the martyrdom of Stephen, many of the followers of Jesus fled the Jerusalem area. Philip, one of the deacons, went to Samaria and there began to make converts. Shortly after this, following a vision, Peter began to accept Gentiles into the new Way, beginning with the centurion Cornelius. Starting here we begin to notice a marked shift in the community's understanding of salvation. God seemed to be doing something new. Heretics and Gentiles were being called to faith in Jesus. If the faith community's discernment was correct, they were being asked to move away from a longstanding view of the exclusivity of Jewish election.

There had long been a universalist position in Judaism. We find it throughout the chapters of Deutero-Isaiah (Isaiah, chapters 40-55), and it becomes the central point in the Book of Jonah. Yet overall in the sacred literature of Israel, the position that God called all nations to salvation represented the minority. Even for those who accepted a universalist position, it was more or less understood that this would entail the nations of the earth coming to *accept Judaism*, to embrace the Covenant and the Law. But some of the Christian apostles were now encouraging Gentiles to embrace Jesus as Lord and Messiah, and the Law was all but ignored in the process.

Such was the case with Paul and Barnabas. In their missionary work they went first to the Jews of the Diaspora, but in the face of rejection they turned to the Gentiles. What they discovered was that the Gentiles were hungry for God's word. Enthusiastically, they began to baptize Gentile converts and set up Christian communities that included Jews and Gentiles alike. In doing so they did not ask their converts to accept all of the Judaic religion as well.

The stage was now set for a dispute within the Christian community that would change not only the constitution of the Church, but also its very structure. Some Jewish Christians from Judea came to Antioch, where Paul and Barnabas were, and began to instruct the community that it was necessary to accept the Mosaic Law, including circumcision, in order to be saved. From a Jewish point of view, this position represented a longstanding principle. There was, after all, the matter of the Covenant and the relationship with God that the Law represented. Gentile converts should accept the complete Mosaic Law. Paul and Barnabas vehemently disagreed. Something new was happening, and it was placing unnecessary burdens upon Gentile converts to ask them to take on all of the Law's demands. The impasse was resolved in the decision to take the matter to the apostolic community at Jerusalem.

The resolution of this early difficulty is given to us in an idealized form in Acts 15, and Paul gives his own brief account as well in Gal 2:1-10. In the longer account in Acts we find Peter speaking as an apostle to the Gentiles. His basic point is that in the action of the Spirit, God showed no distinction between Jews and Gentiles. James, speaking as the head of the Jerusalem community, and possibly a central figure on the traditionalist side, basically supports this position while counseling for a few reasonable exceptions. It is his position that the community ultimately agrees upon. The outcome of this Church council was to agree that the Law was not to be considered mandatory for the Christian faith, at least for the non-Jew. The few elements of the Law that remained universally in force were mostly seen as being necessary for everyone for genuine worship.

What is not recorded in the account of Acts 15, but what the leaders of the Church must have known, was just how much was at stake for the future of the Church. For many believers, to be a follower of Christ was also to accept the basic understanding of God's Covenant love, which in their minds implied following the Law. By what right could this be done away with? Moreover, the Gospel was not accepted by the Gentiles in a vacuum. They had come to believe in the context of their own pagan culture and social customs. In light of the predominant Jewish position that these pagan cultures were excluded from God's election, how could the social customs of these cultures now be acceptable? It was not, after all, a question of the Law or nothing. If they didn't have to follow the social customs of the Law, what social customs would they follow? The only ones left were the norms and customs of their own pagan background. To mitigate the Law meant to sanction the position that the Christian faith and pagan social customs were not inimical, that the pagan population, along with its social norms and laws, was fertile ground for proclaiming God's Word.

It cannot be supposed that the decision of the Jerusalem council was arrived at lightly. It reversed a well-entrenched Jewish mentality, but even more, it established a position of the Church early on that would have its impact on every Christian henceforth: that the Gospel of Jesus Christ would find its home in every culture and every social milieu, that it would use the given culture to proclaim its message of salvation, and that it would allow the culture to help form the context in which the Gospel was transmitted. While this was a departure from the predominant Jewish norms that the Church was born into, it was not seen as a betrayal of the message of Jesus, and in fact was interpreted as a means of carrying out the Christian mission.

It is interesting to note that in 50 A.D., approximately when the Jerusalem gathering took place, no part of what became the New Testament was yet in written form. What the leaders of the community had available to them were the many stories and remembrances of Jesus, their faith in and experience of the Resurrection of Jesus, their knowledge of the liturgical and confessional formulas presently in use in the community, and their discernment of how the Spirit of Jesus was calling them to act. Their decision in this case and in many others yet to come was based primarily on what had been handed on to them, a criterion that has come to be known as Tradition. Some present-day Christians hold that Scripture is the sole criterion for how life in the Church should look, yet this most fateful of decisions, one to which most Christians stand indebted, took place totally outside of our recorded Scripture. In fact, it is safe to say that the form Scripture itself took was highly influenced by the decision.

What the early experience of the Church demonstrates is how much it has always been open to accepting non-Christian influences in its shaping of the context in which the Gospel is proclaimed (just as in reality Judaism was before it, though indirectly[2]). What was understood and accepted by the Jerusalem Council more formally has subsequently happened informally innumerable times in the Church's history. There has never been a time when the Christian community was not in some way incorporating elements from the cultures around it. We need only look at the development of ministry and office within the Church to see how the faith community took on more Greek and Roman hierarchical structures. The same is true with its liturgical structure, as well as its feasts

---

[2] We might recall in this regard the voice of the Pharisee Gamaliel (Acts 5:34-39), who counseled for a test of fruitfulness in discerning the innovation of the followers of Jesus.

(after all, even Christmas was originally a pagan celebration in honor of the rebirth of the invincible sun). There is no clearer example of non-Christian influence in the Church than in its philosophical and theological thought. Thomism, for example, the Christian philosophical structure dominant for centuries, is primarily based on the principles of pagan Aristotelianism and greatly influenced by Arabian writings.

Of course, my diversion here from an exploration of conversion has as its context the Enneagram. Sometimes I hear the complaint that it comes from a non-Christian source. We will explore its roots more completely in the next chapter, but it is safe to agree that in the narrowest sense the Enneagram did not arise from within a Christian context. Yet it is not a criticism at all to say this. The real question is not where it comes from, but how do we evaluate it and discern its fruitfulness in light of our faith in the Scripture and the apostolic Tradition of the Church. These have always been the criteria for accepting what was beyond the community's experience. In effect, that is one of the primary reasons for this book, to explore the Enneagram from within a Christian faith context. It is my contention that this context can be found within a theology of conversion, and to this I once again turn.

CONVERSION IN THE CHURCH

From all scriptural evidence conversion was a part of the Church's experience from the beginning.

It was a key piece of the basic message of faith, the *kērygma*, as pictured in the early chapters of the Acts of the Apostles. The evangelist Luke places the call to conversion on the lips of Peter on the very day of Pentecost. "Repent and be baptized, every one of you, in the name of Jesus Christ for the forgiveness of your sins; and you will receive the gift of the holy Spirit." (Acts 2:38) Again and again in the early speeches, meant to convey the essential structure of the community's faith, the apostles urge conversion,[3] and speak of Jesus' death as a means for the forgiveness of sin.[4]

It is important to note that, even from the earliest of speeches recorded in Acts 2, conversion is linked with the action of baptism. Baptism was seen to be the mark of the true follower of Christ, the concrete sign of the individual's belief in the death, resurrection, and lordship of Jesus. It was understood by the early community of faith that baptism brought about what even the many sin offerings in the Temple in Jerusalem never claimed to accomplish, not simply the expiation of sin, but the actual forgiveness of sin, a prerogative reserved only for God.

Baptism was understood to bring about a total and complete transformation of the believer, affecting every aspect of life, the means of salvation in Christ. "Or are you unaware that we who were baptized into Christ Jesus were baptized into his death? We were

---

[3] Acts 3:19; 17:30.

[4] Acts 5:31; 10:43; 13:38.

indeed buried with him through baptism into death, so that, just as Christ was raised from the dead by the glory of the Father, we too might live in newness of life." (Romans 6:3-4) This is reiterated in the First Letter of Peter.

> Blessed be the God and Father of our Lord Jesus Christ, who in his great mercy gave us a new birth to a living hope through the resurrection of Jesus Christ from the dead, to an inheritance that is imperishable, undefiled, and unfading, kept in heaven for you who by the power of God are safeguarded through faith, to a salvation that is ready to be revealed in the final time. (1 Peter 1:3-5)

The one who received baptism was to truly become a new reality. "So whoever is in Christ is a new creation: the old things have passed away; behold, new things have come." (2 Cor 5:17)

The call to conversion in the early Church was at its heart a call to faith, for human sinfulness was intricately bound to unbelief. This was no less true for the Jews than it was for the Gentiles. For Jews the Church focused this unbelief on the rejection of Jesus. For Gentiles the call to conversion was a demand that they leave behind their pagan idolatry. Paul claims in Acts of the Apostles, "And I did not at all shrink from telling you what was for your benefit, or from teaching you in public or in your homes. I earnestly bore witness for both Jews and Greeks to repentance before God and to faith in our Lord Jesus.' (Acts 20:20-21)

Baptism was, in the beginning, essentially an adult experience. It was the adult individual who, confronted with the hopelessness of his or her sin, was to freely embrace the new life offered in Christ. However, as we can see from the experience of Peter with Cornelius in Acts 10, it was natural that whole households would seek to receive baptism. Still, repentance was understood as a conscious choice, a total restructuring of values and behaviors around this new core experience, belief in salvation through the Risen Jesus.

The reception of baptism was understood to be a once-and-for-all experience. Like discipleship, which it symbolized, there was no turning back once one had set out upon the path. The Christian was not expected to lapse into serious sin again, and the structures for dealing with such an occurence were by and large nonexistent. Paul's solution, for instance, for a serious moral problem in the community at Corinth was expulsion from the Church (1 Cor 5:2).

Of course, sinfulness of a lesser sort continued to exist among Christians. Disputes and disagreements, factions, misunderstandings, and mistreatment of one another happened as they would be expected to. The place where these less serious transgressions were rectified was at the eucharistic table. Before the bread was broken and shared, the assembly was called to be at one, and early communities developed simple rituals for the general acknowledgement of sinfulness and the expression of peace among the membership.

CONVERSION IN PROCESS

As the Church continued to grow and spread around the Mediterranean basin and beyond, the understanding of conversion continued to develop. The initial contacts with Greek and Latin culture increased as the Christian community became more and more a non-Jewish phenomenon. In many ways the impact of the wider culture of the Roman Empire represented a positive development in the Church. At other times, however, the stance of the faith community was necessarily counter to the culture that surrounded it. Often the early Church underwent persecutions at the hands of the Roman or local governments. If anything, however, these times seemed to solidify the belief of the Church, and in the end actually strengthened it. Conversion to faith in the Risen Christ often meant the new Christian literally placed his or her life on the line.

Baptism was the definitive means of the forgiveness of sin, and the Christian life was to be totally new. While sinful behavior would no doubt continue to some extent, it was understood that a primary choice had been made. However, the early persecutions created a new pastoral problem for the Church. When the turmoil ended and a relative peace had returned, it frequently happened that individuals who, in the face of possible death, had denied their faith, would then seek readmission into the community. This denial had cut these individuals off from the Church. What could now be done with them? Some favored a rebaptism, but most seemed to feel there was no way this could happen. Baptism, after all, was itself a death and resurrection, and it would therefore seem to be unrepeatable. On the other hand, the attitude of Jesus in the gospels seemed to mandate that somehow forgiveness should be extended to those who sincerely wished to return.

Other sins of a very public nature were also surfacing in the various communities. Sins such as adultery, murder, and idolatry were also felt to be very serious, and in some way cut the individuals involved off from the faith community. Just as with apostasy, their very nature seemed to be a denial of what had been claimed at baptism. How could the Church seek to embody the compassion of Jesus, and still maintain the integrity of the radical nature of baptism?

It was only gradually that the Church came to develop an understanding of how to reincorporate members who had gravely and publicly sinned. This process came to be embodied in the practice of public penance. The sinner stood before the bishop, who spoke for the local community, and confessed the sin that had been committed. The individual would then be admitted to the order of penitents. The community's penitents, like its catechumens, would be excluded from receiving the Eucharist but would be present for the liturgy of the Word. Their status as penitents would remain in effect until the bishop and the community deemed the penitent worthy to be readmitted to the full life of the Church. Then the bishop would impose hands upon the penitent as a sign of forgiveness.

While in the Order of Penitents, for a period of time that varied with circumstances from place to place, the repentant sinner was expected to demonstrate concretely an internal attitude of repentance. This was done through many forms of mortification, some of them severe, some prolonged. Fasting, almsgiving, and prayer were among the more frequently prescribed. Abstention from sexual relations during the time of penance was also expected. Moreover, following certain careers was not permitted to penitents, such as serving in the military, being a merchant, and holding public office.

This public penance was the first form of what came to be called the Sacrament of Reconciliation or Confession. In its development the Church was recognizing an important fact about conversion; that is, that conversion was not always a once-and-for-all experience. There was the need through the continual admission of sinfulness in Eucharist and on occasion through the more dramatic public penance to acknowledge that the call to holiness and grace was a lifetime concern.

In these early centuries, however, penance could only be received once. It was felt that such public sins were of a magnitude that required severe treatment. It was not expected that the sincere Christian would continually fail. When it did happen, therefore, harsh measures were felt to be justified. Often they lasted for years, and sometimes contained stipulations that continued for the rest of the penitent's life.

This was all meant to convey the sacrament's importance, thereby building a reverence for it, but in time it began to have the opposite effect. Because of the severity of the penitential disciplines, there was a growing tendency to delay entrance into the Order of

Penitents. Eventually it became something to put off until one was close to death. Entering the Order of Penitents became less and less frequent, so that by the sixth century public penance had basically fallen into disuse. With fewer Christians seeking to enter it before they were near death, public canonical penance had practically no real impact on the lives of most members of the Church. The penitential disciplines became more and more a way of life taken up on a voluntary basis by Christians who were seeking a more rigorous spirituality. As a sacramental structure they were essentially ineffective.[5]

At the same time, however, a new pastoral practice was being introduced by Celtic monks, serving

---

[5] As the Order of Penitents came to consist almost exclusively of individuals who had freely entered its discipline, this voluntary movement took on a new vitality along different lines. The Order of Penance continued as a grass roots movement into the Middle Ages, where it adapted itself to the spirituality of some of the Church's greatest spiritual figures, such as Francis of Assisi and Dominic of Caleruega. Known as Third Orders, these associations continued to have an impact upon the Church into the present. In the Franciscan tradition the Order of Penance continues in the many Secular Franciscan associations, and in the context of formal religious life in the male and female communities of the Third Order Regular. For more detail in regard to its historical development see: Pazzelli, Raphael. *St. Francis and the Third Order.* Chicago: Franciscan Herald Press, 1989.

as missionaries throughout Europe.[6] The new practice departed from the form of public penance in several important ways.   First, in place of a long indefinite period of harsh disciplines, the monks introduced specific acts of penance correlated with particular sins committed. These were included in small books called "Penitentials." Secondly, forgiveness of sin was offered not only by the bishop, but also now by the monks who were spreading the practice throughout Europe, making penance much more accessible. Third, the forum for penance shifted from the public life of the community to the privacy between penitent and confessor. And most importantly, the new penance could be received an indefinite number of times. There was no longer the need to delay penance lest one would again slip into sin. Now there was the growing recognition that an ongoing confrontation with sinfulness was part of the normal Christian life.

With the development of frequent receptions of penance, a new understanding of sin and conversion had taken hold.   In one sense it reaffirmed the ongoing nature of conversion.   As we shall see, this was connected to the practice of infant baptism, which was already in universal use by the time the peniten-

---

[6] This practice introduced by the monks grew out of the private spiritual direction taking place within the monasteries. It did not originally include what we now understand as a sacramental absolution.   Its development evolved to fill the gap left by the collapse of canonical penance.

tials were introduced. The faith community needed a tangible way to pursue ongoing conversion since baptism was no longer the dramatic choice for Christ by the adult believer. However, in the mechanical listing of penances for particular sinful actions we can already find the seed of future problems. The tendency would be for conversion to become more and more solidified into objective ritual. As this took place, real interior change of heart became further removed from the process.

THE TENDENCY TO SIN

It was clear in the early Church, as it is to us as well, that our understanding of sin must necessarily embrace realities much deeper than surface behaviors. We know this from our own experiences, recognizing in those moments of clarity the intricate web that entangles us in destructive behavior -- destructive of ourselves, and others as well -- and stretches deep into the layers of our personality. So the early faith community also recognized that beneath the identifiable behavioral patterns of sin something else was present. There was within human nature a kind of inclination to sin.

In the earliest writings of the Church the apostle Paul had introduced an awareness of this. Particularly in his letter to the Romans, where Paul seeks to present his understanding of moral justification in the Christian life, we can see how he understood the deeply rooted nature of our sinfulness. Paul attempts to explain how we as Christians come to justification, or moral righteousness.

In the Jewish tradition justification was understood in two different ways. While not mutually exclusive, different scriptural traditions tended to favor one or the other.[7] The first view, which was the predominant view of Scripture, was that one is justified by one's own ethical behavior. The Law presented God's moral will, and to perform the works of the Law made a person righteous before God. The second view, however, held that human righteousness before God was not possible. We are justified by God's grace, and not by our works. Paul was taught in the ways of the former view, and its effect still had an impact on his thinking, as can be seen in Romans 2:5-13. But the experience of conversion had given Paul a completely new perspective on God's grace. It is this second view of justification that Paul seeks to present in his letter to the Church at Rome.

In the first chapters of Romans Paul goes to great lengths to emphasize that all people are under the sway of sin, both the Jews and the non-Jews. The Law of Moses has not kept the people of the Covenant from sharing in what Paul paints as a universal dominance of sinful forces. In Chapter 5 he uses the already existing Jewish midrash of Adam to explain how sin had entered the world at the very beginning of human life. In the same way, all people carried this inclination to sin with them. Even though the

---

[7] See: Schillebeeckx, Edward. *Christ: The Experience of Jesus as Lord.* New York: The Seabury Press, 1980. pp.126-159.

nature of sin might not have been recognized, still it was present.

> Therefore, just as through one person sin entered the world, and through sin, death, and thus death came to all, inasmuch as all sinned -- for up to the time of the law, sin was in the world, though sin is not accounted where there is no law. But death reigned from Adam to Moses, even over those who did not sin after the pattern of the trespass of Adam, who is the type of the one who was to come. (Romans 5:12-14)

With the coming of the Mosaic Law sin became, as it were, conscious, that is, recognizable. But in one sense this recognition made matters worse. Now sin could be named, and human responsibility for sinful actions therefore increased.

> What then can we say? That the law is sin? Of course not! Yet I did not know sin except through the law, and I did not know what it is to covet except that the law said, "You shall not covet." But sin, finding an opportunity in the commandment, produced in me every kind of covetousness. Apart from the law sin is dead. (Romans 7:7-8)

Paul is not seeking to blame the Law for his own actions; nor is he saying that the Law in itself is evil.

But he is saying something significant about the process whereby we come to life in God. While an understanding of the Law revealed to Paul (and here he is speaking for all) much of the nature of sinfulness, it could not in itself *free* him from sinfulness. Here to some extent we can see Paul reflecting on his own experiences, for using the Law to attain his own righteousness before God was the very approach that the pre-conversion Saul had tried to use.[8] In his own estimation all he did was become a slave to his own quest for perfection. The Law was not evil, but Paul's own sinful inclinations used what was intended as good and turned it upside down. "We know that the law is spiritual; but I am carnal, sold into slavery to sin. What I do, I do not understand. For I do not do what I want, but I do what I hate." (Romans 7:14-15)

Fortunately for Paul (and for us as well), there is a power beyond the Law. The Law, after all, could offer expiation for sin, ways of "making up" for what one did, but it could not extend forgiveness. That was reserved for God alone. But the power beyond human legislation, a power initiated specifically by God, was found in the triumph of Jesus over death. In our faith in Christ's victory, and in our *action* of faith through baptism, we come to justification of our sinfulness.

Hence, now there is no condemnation for those who are in Christ Jesus. For the law of the spirit of life in Christ Jesus has freed

---

[8] See: Philippians 3:4-11.

you from the law of sin and death. For what the law, weakened by the flesh, was powerless to do, this God has done: by sending his own Son in the likeness of sinful flesh and for the sake of sin, he condemned sin in the flesh, so that the righteous decree of the law might be fulfilled in us, who live not according to the flesh but according to the spirit. (Romans 8:1-4)

Of course, Paul did not mean to imply that the ritual act of baptism was some kind of automatic "quick fix" for sin. Faith was not simply a matter of performing an external ceremony and then continuing unchanged in one's previous lifestyle.[9] Paul urges the believer not to return to what was left behind in baptism. Using the concept of flesh, *sarx*, to signify the human person standing alone, unconnected to God, Paul warns the believers:

For if you live according to the flesh, you will die, but if by the spirit you put to death the deeds of the body, you will live. For those who are led by the Spirit of God are children of God. For you did not receive a spirit of slavery to fall back into fear, but you received a spirit of adoption, through which we cry, "*Abba*, Father!" (Romans 8:13-15)

---

[9] Here Paul could be said to be in agreement with the Letter of James. See James 2:14-26.

So there was in the early Church the recognition, born out of experience --Paul's as well as so many others who were attempting to live the faith -- of the presence of an inclination toward sinfulness in our very human constitution. It was an inclination that the structures of legally oriented religions could point out, but themselves had no power over. A holistic faith in the Resurrected Christ, confirmed in baptism, and lived out each day in action toward the Reign of God, asserted power over sin's inclination, but the effects of our sinful nature remained to the extent that our lives were not lived in conformity with Christ.

The widespread acknowledgement of this tendency toward sin is attested to in the increasingly common practice of infant baptism. If there was no acceptance of our inclination to sin, why would the faith community have wished to baptize children soon after birth? The child had obviously made no conscious choice to depart from God. It would seem that real moral choice was not yet possible for one so young. But there was a growing sense of the need to baptize children as soon after birth as possible.

The rationale for this developed slowly in the early centuries and came to be solidified in the doctrine of original sin. In turn, once original sin was well established in its theological context, it had the effect of making infant baptism a universal phenomenon in the Church. The primary shaping of the doctrine came at the hands of Augustine. He took as his starting point an idea originally proposed by Cyprian of Carthage over a century before, that children, even though not old enough to actually commit sin, were still guilty of the inherited sin of

Adam. Cyprian had based his idea on the words of Paul in Romans (5:12-21). Augustine expanded on the idea by maintaining that Adam's sin was passed on from one generation to the next by the father in human procreation (consistent with the contemporary belief that life was passed on solely by the father's seed). Original sin was within each of us from birth. It was necessary, then, for our salvation to receive baptism so that we could be reshaped from this essential deformity of soul into a new conformity with Christ.

However, to fully understand Augustine's position on original sin, it is necessary to recognize that it developed in dialectic with an opposing theological position held by the British monk Pelagius. It seemed to Pelagius that Augustine, in maintaining the position that without God's grace sin was unavoidable, had taken too extreme a stance. We could claim not to be morally responsible for our actions because God had withheld grace. Why bother to act righteously if it was not in our power to avoid sin at all? So Pelagius proposed a state of "original grace." Adam's sin merely lost for us a "grace of pardon," which was restored by Christ. However, this left Pelagius in a position of needing to defend how Christ's grace was necessary for salvation at all. Augustine, in taking the opposing position of "original sin," was able to maintain the Church's view that we could not be saved without the redemption of Christ.[10]

That the extreme position of Pelagius would be rejected by the Church is perhaps not so surprising. That Augustine's relatively negative stance toward human nature should receive such overwhelming acceptance by the Church, especially in the West, might, however, cause us some wonder. Yet the doctrine of original sin came at a time when historical factors in Europe seemed to enhance its credibility.

The Edict of Milan in 313 had officially legitimized the Christian religion within the Roman Empire. By 380 it had become the empire's official religion. While these actions had their share of positive effects upon the Church, they also presented some clearly negative features. The level of moral quality in the average Christian fell noticeably. It no longer took something extra to be a Christian. Now one could follow Christ in name without effectively changing lifestyle. This watered-down picture of Christianity drove many away from established Christian communities into the desert, where they chose to do spiritual battle with the forces of evil in solitude.

At the same time Christianity was watching the slow unraveling and collapse of the most advanced

---

[10] For a more complete historical treatment of the question of original sin in the context of the sacrament of baptism, see: Martos, Joseph. *Doors To the Sacred: A Historical Introduction to Sacraments in the Catholic Church.* Garden City, NY: Doubleday & Co, Inc., 1982. pp. 174-178.

culture then known. The Roman Empire was crumbling before the Church's very eyes. Inside, the empire was ruled by people who were less and less capable of governing, who sometimes showed obvious signs of insanity. Outside, waves of "barbarians" were overwhelming all that was understood to be civilized. While these tribal people might eventually submit to Christianity, they were still imbued with what seemed to the Church to be the most shocking of customs.

Europe was plunging into the Dark Ages, where it seemed its very social and cultural network was being shattered. The Church, in its theological reflection, looked around at the evolving situation of the world, and came to the view that humanity was fundamentally flawed and depraved. Most social structures other than those of the Church had collapsed, and it seemed that humanity needed maximum discipline to curb its insatiable appetite for things that the Christian was supposed to reject.

Although culture would eventually emerge once again from the darkness, it would be a slow and agonizing process. In the face of a vastly uneducated Europe, the theological pessimism concerning human righteousness remained intact. While original sin might be defined as a "fall from grace," any sense of where humanity might have fallen *from* was downplayed to the point of neglect. The sense of an original call and destiny that was once more tangibly offered to us in Christ, while of course upheld in theory, was lost in the midst of theological pessimism and apparent historical experience.[11] The tendency to sin had come to outweigh, in theological focus, the realization of creation's inherent goodness, and more energy was spent pointing to the depravity of human nature than reinforcing its essential giftedness by God.

CONVERSION IN STASIS

The confluence of factors that were emerging in the Church's conception of repentance and sinfulness -- namely, the theological pessimism over human righteousness, the emphasis on the doctrine of original sin, and the increasingly automatic nature of ritualized reconciliation -- had the effect of bringing to the Church a more and more static understanding of conversion. Through the Middle Ages and down into the Modern era, the sacrament of penance, which in the Roman Church became the sole locus of conversion, came to be understood and experienced in a very strict and formal manner.

As European culture began to stabilize during the Middle Ages, there was a re-emergence of intellectual development in the Christian experience. First, the great monasteries, and then the emerging universities, began to produce philosophers and

---

[11] The desire to correct the balance between this pessimistic view of humanity and a more fundamental optimism is at the heart of the Creation-centered spirituality movement. See, for instance: Fox, Matthew. *Original Blessing*. Santa Fe, NM: Bear & Company, 1983.

thinkers who once more sought to explore the deeper problems of human nature. Drawing heavily from Aristolelian thought, particularly as it had been disseminated through learning centers in the Arabic world, Christian philosophers began to develop new approaches to philosophy and human reason. Theology was understood as being approachable through, though not encompassed by, philosophical structures. Scholastic philosophy and theology slowly became the accepted, and then the undisputed, context out of which the Western Church sought to express its faith.

Moral theology, which had lain dormant for 400 years, once more became a focus of interest in the Scholastic period. What was already largely categorical in practice through the circulating penitentials became even more solidified through the unyielding categories of systematic thought. For instance, in the work of Thomas Aquinas, the leading voice of the Scholastic period, the lines separating mortal sin and venial sin became well established. Virtues and vices were human habitual behaviors that could be evaluated solely through human reason. Virtues were clearly distinguished as moral or intellectual, cardinal, theological, and so forth. Perfection became a matter of absolute attributes residing by nature only in God. Nature and supernature were finely delineated as all life was subjected to Aristotle's metaphysical duality.

As the Church sought to develop its pastoral approach within a Scholastic framework, there was a growing emphasis on behaviorally focused morality. Sin was act-oriented, and an emphasis came to be placed on quantitative measurement. It was supposed that sin carried with it the necessity of punishment;

that a satisfaction for sinful behavior could be expected. Whereas initially this punishment had been satisfied in the penitential disciplines of public penance, these "temporal punishments" were increasingly "commuted" to prayers and other devotions that were thought to meet a similar satisfaction. Gradually there grew up a system of indulgences that themselves were seen in a very act-centered way.

Thus ongoing conversion, biblical *metanoia*, came to be reduced to a kind of spiritual barter system. The Christian was to "make penance" and "perform penances" so that satisfaction could be accomplished. Of course, the *sacrament* of penance, or confession, was the sole arena where this could be done. After the Council of Trent in the 16th century, the Roman church, which was attempting to restructure following the Reformation, imposed a definite and static format on the sacrament, as it did on the entire sacramental system. From that time on, the mechanical features of sin and forgiveness were clearly in place.

Following the Reformation, the word "conversion" became more and more identified with switching religious affiliation, and not with a fundamental call to transform one's life in keeping with the Gospel. Any sense of conversion as a life process that would lead to holiness was relegated more or less completely to what was called the field of ascetical theology. Here it used the language not of conversion, but of *purgation*.

The purgative way named the first of three hierarchic paths to God. In the purgative way one was to purge the self of sinfulness, vices, and inordinate attachments. This was followed by entering into the second way of perfection, the way of illumination, where one sought to acquire virtue, and pursue the means to spiritual wisdom. The third path to perfection, the unitive way, then led the individual to a total immersion in God, characterized by infused contemplative prayer. In one of the earliest theological treatments of the three ways, Bonaventure, in the mid-13th century, presented them as three concurrent movements of the spiritual life. However, by the time of the ascetical manuals of the early 20th century the three spiritual ways had become more or less static stages of spiritual development. When one entered into illumination, it was presumed that for the most part the need for purgation was left behind. Since in practice few people felt they had truly left purgation behind, the system tended to foster a rather constant requestioning of oneself and of one's experiences.

By the mid-20th century, the end result of all these developments was a spiritual regime that had a very clear understanding of sinfulness and forgiveness, of holiness and ascetical discipline, and of spiritual growth. It was, however, also very rigid and perfectionistic, and it used a language that was increasingly less able to speak to the emerging spiritual concerns of men and women. Any understanding of penance (for the word "conversion" no longer fit well in the context) was almost totally sacramental. It was seen either as an obligation that, if done unworthily, could bring down condemnation rather than forgiveness upon the penitent, or as one more piety that would accrue "merit" for the devout believer. All this was set in the context of a highly introverted spirituality primarily developed within the formative structures of religious life. Few Catholics heard much of the three spiritual ways, for it was presumed that most "average Christians" would be remaining in the purgative way. The stage was essentially set for the series of revolutionary changes that have swept our understanding of spirituality in the last 30 to 40 years.

CONVERSION AS PROCESS

The Second Vatican Council did not just spring up out of a vacuum. Although many of the faithful, who had come to see their Church as a stable and never-changing entity, were surprised and even shocked at the widespread changes of Vatican II, the Council was a response to factors that had long been crying out to be addressed. The horrors visited upon Europe and the world by Nazism and the Second World War, the rapidly expanding technology of the world community, the reality of militarism gone unchecked, and the growing realization that the world was becoming a global community all called for the Church to speak in new ways. The biblical movement, the liturgical movement, and the ecumenical movement all needed some kind of formal structural channels in order that they might proceed with greater fruitfulness.   The Council's documents, while they were truly works of tremendous innovation, were the result of years of foundational work in theology and morality.

In the years following the Council, theologians sought to build on its documentation in order to re-envision every field of theology. Moral theologians were faced with a complex world that would have been unimaginable to Thomas Aquinas or Alphonsus Liguori. Nuclear war, genetic engineering, racial and social discrimination, and multinational economics had created new problems that demanded totally fresh treatment. It seemed to many that the old categories of sin paled before these new social developments, and many sought to find a new basis for understanding sin. In general these new trends centered around the difference between sin understood as an act and sin understood as an attitude.

Moral theologians in the post-Vatican II Church developed the concept of "fundamental option" as a new approach to sinfulness. Every person through the course of his or her life was making a fundamental choice, either toward God and faith or away from God. This fundamental option was a life orientation, a choice more easily seen in the wider view than in the isolated act. Mortal sin was understood as what severed a relationship with God, and which had to be measured more by one's overall stance toward life than by an individual incident.

The basic criticism of this attitudinal approach was that some could use it to discount the significance of an individual action. However, in general, the concept of fundamental option was a very positive development, for it affirmed the growing realization that sin was not to be seen as an isolated reality. A totally act-centered understanding of sinfulness had created a mentality that saw sins as so many bad pennies. They could be stacked on top of each other or examined individually, but objectively their value never changed and their weight depended to a great extent upon their quantity. Instead of this, there was now a call to see sin as an entwining web, an interconnected labyrinth, and holiness as a process or a movement toward God.

The understanding of conversion as well has slowly been restructured. As recently as a generation ago, conversion was still understood by most Roman Catholics to mean the switching from one religion to another. Since the Vatican Council, the biblical movement has fortunately set the stage for recapturing a Gospel understanding of conversion. But even now there is a tendency among Christians, mainline and evangelical alike, to understand conversion as an *experience.* We hear the language of making a choice for God, of accepting Jesus as our personal Lord and Savior. We imagine Paul struck down on the road to Damascus and match it to our own experience of the altar call, the parish mission, the 30-day retreat, or the baptism of the spirit. But if sin is a process that pulls us down to our own degradation, then what stands opposite sin -- conversion -- must be explored as a call to another kind of process, the process toward faith and holiness.

As a process, conversion is primarily life directional, not only an experience but a complete attitudinal thrust of one's whole life. Just as the process of sinfulness can encompass intense experiences, choices, and actions that retard our growth and sever our relationship with God (for individual actions *are* in fact significant in understanding sin), so the process of conversion can have dramatic and intense moments as well. Conversion as a process does not seek to minimalize that experience during the 30-day retreat or the dramatic event of the baptism of the spirit. It does, however, acknowledge that to sustain the important conversion events we experience, we must find ways of fitting them into the larger context of our lives. They must be reinforced by the ongoing nature of our life choices.

In presenting this understanding of the conversion and sin processes within us, I realize I am using a language that much of the contemporary world has stopped listening to. *Conversion* is a word that seems to be irrelevant to all but the religious-minded, and the synonyms for conversion -- repentance and penance -- carry many unfortunate connotations even to those who are oriented toward the spiritual. But even more than these, the word *sin* conjures up all sorts of memories of past abberations, negative baggage from the religious education of our youth, that make it very difficult to hear with an open attitude.

By and large, the psychological community is *most* uncomfortable with the concept of sin, but even some circles of theology that in recent decades have been highly influenced by contemporary psychology do their best to shun the treatment of sinfulness whenever possible. This is in part a reaction to centuries of a Christian/European overemphasis on sinfulness, and a tendency, as has been mentioned, to view humanity as innately perverse. Much of the psychological world, particularly in its Freudian and behaviorist schools, adds to this its own "hands off" approach to anything spiritual. God and anything directly related to God cannot be addressed or explored. God, after all, is not a good subject for scientific method. It must be noted, however, that there are schools of psychology, for instance, the Jungians and what is referred to as transpersonal psychology, that feel some freedom to explore what lies beyond the realm of human measurement. It is my hope that as the spiritual and the psychological continue to grow together a greater mutual acceptance and understanding will result. What is to me the strangest feature in this avoidance of the language of sinfulness is that psychology itself, from its very inception as a science, has felt the need to enter into the darker side of human existence. In so doing it is my perception that many psychological schools do little better than their pre-psychological counterparts in painting a positive picture of humanity. Many of the founders of psychological movements began by looking at abnormal and destructive human behavior, and their models have often tended to flow from their focus of attention. Immature and unhealthy behavior is laid out through character disorders, neuroses, psychotic episodes, pathological tendencies, ego dysfunctions, and so on. It is strange that a small word like *sin* should put off so many.

Therefore, in presenting conversion as an ongoing life process, I must ask the reader to make a kind of jump, and in the process to let go of some past presuppositions. For those who approach this book from a religious or spiritual framework, I ask you not to fear psychological terminology. For those who come from the perspective of the human sciences, I ask you to face squarely the possibility that spirituality is not an enemy, and that theological expression can be an extremely accurate means of articulating human experience.

SIN AS CONSCIOUS ACTION AND MINDLESS ADDICTION

The reality of sin has been presented and understood in many ways. From the writings of the Old Testament, through the New Testament, and down through the centuries of the Church, many images and conceptual frameworks have been offered, with wide variation. In a general way, however, our understanding of sin has pointed to some kind of conscious choice against God. And in that general understanding of sin it has been accepted that the individual has some level of accountability for one's actions. We cannot disregard this conclusion. It is a conclusion born out of the lived experience of our human journey; it is attested to through the ages. Even if much of what is said in this section will seem to mitigate personal responsibility for our sinfulness, we cannot escape the reality of that responsibility, nor would we want to.

Jesus understood that we were accountable for our actions. He says in the Sermon on the Mount, "Therefore, whoever breaks one of the least of these commandments and teaches others to do so will be called least in the kingdom of heaven. But whoever obeys and teaches these commandments will be called greatest in the kingdom of heaven." (Mt 5:19) He reproached the local towns of Galilee for their choosing to reject his message of the Kingdom (Lk 10:13-16). The fruitfulness that we bear or don't bear will depend by and large on the kind of people we are.

> You brood of vipers, how can you say good things when you are evil? For from the fullness of the heart the mouth speaks. A good person brings forth good out of a store of goodness, but an evil person brings forth evil out of a store of evil. I tell you, on the day of judgment people will render an account for every careless word they speak. By your words you will be acquitted, and by your words you will be condemned. (Mt 12:34-37)

Yet Jesus fully understood the complexity of our human nature, and he knew how easily we become trapped and enmeshed in actions and behaviors that go far beyond our limited awareness of what we are actually doing. Also in the Sermon on the Mount Jesus contrasts the results of good and bad spiritual vision. If I see well, my whole being will be filled with light, but a distorted vision has tremendous ramifications, for my whole being will be enveloped in darkness. And if what I come to see as light is in reality darkness, "how great will the darkness be." (Mt 6:22-23)

We can reflect on the parable of the two sons and the forgiving father (Lk 15:11-32) to see how easily our actions can rise from a source we are not in the least aware of. The younger son believes he is doing good, claiming his independence, taking responsibility for what he considers his own. It is only when he finally is sitting among the pigs that he realizes the true nature of his actions. The older brother presents his "case" to the father. He did everything right --

"not once did I disobey your orders" -- but he fails to see the jealousy and the mistrust of his relationship with his father that lie beneath his feelings of righteousness. We have explored the call to compassion that Jesus places before us. It arises in part from his awareness of how easy it is for us to deceive ourselves.

There is a growing awareness in our society of the truly overwhelming nature of addictive behavior. Whether it is dependency on alcohol or drugs, on work, on sexuality, or on one of the intricate networks of enabling relationships that so universally accompany them, our society is discovering how very easy it is to trade in our freedom for an illusion. Whereas the Twelve-Step Program, begun with Alcoholics Anonymous, has been around for many years, much more recently its wisdom has spread to other types of dependencies and co-dependencies. Moreover, it is only a very recent development that contemporary writers have begun to approach an understanding of sin from the point of view of addiction.[12] To me this new awareness is very helpful. In completing my overview of the theological development of conversion, I would like to draw from some of the ideas presented by Gerald May, a psychiatrist who is the Director for Research & Program Development at the Shalem Institute in Washington, DC, found in his book *Addiction and Grace.*

---

[12] See: McCormick, Patrick. *Sin As Addiction.* New York: Paulist Press, 1989.; also: May, Gerald G. *Addiction and Grace.* San Francisco: Harper & Row, 1988.

May begins his book by naming the human heart's desire as essentially a desire for God. "After twenty years of listening to the yearnings of people's hearts, I am convinced that all human beings have an inborn desire for God. Whether we are consciously religious or not, this desire is our deepest longing and our most precious treasure."[13] But something has happened to us that keeps us from pursuing that which we most want. We find that our desires are captured, our intentions distorted. This is the experience of sin.

> Theologically, sin is what turns us away from love -- away from love for ourselves, away from love for one another, and away from love for God. When I look at this problem psychologically, I see two forces that are responsible: repression and addiction. We all suffer from both repression and addiction. Of the two, repression is by far the milder one.[14]

Repression stifles desire, attempting to keep it from our awareness. Addiction, however, seeks to substitute something else for our truest desire. May says, "...addiction *attaches* desire, bonds and enslaves the energy of desire to certain specific behaviors, things, or people. These objects of attachment then

---

[13] May, Gerald G. *Addiction and Grace*, p. 1.

[14] May, Gerald G. *Addiction and Grace*. p.2

become preoccupations and obsessions; they come to rule our lives."[15] It is just this bondage, just this enslavement, that gives us the truest nature of sin, the evil that sin is.

It is May's belief, and I echo his position, that we are all addicts. If we are not addicted to drugs and alcohol, we are addicted to power, or approval, or comfort, or consuming, or any number of hundreds of other possibilities. What then are we to understand an addiction to be? May offers a simple definition: "Addiction is any compulsive, habitual behavior that limits the freedom of human desire. It is caused by the attachment, or nailing, of desire to specific objects."[16] Human freedom, then, always stands counter to addictive behavior. If sin is an enslavement, conversion must in some way lead to liberation.

There are two types of addictive behavior that Gerald May proposes. When we first think of addiction to substances like alcohol and drugs, we think of being pulled toward something that initially attracts us. But we must also realize that we can form addictions to things we hope will *keep us from* experiencing something. Here the motive for the addiction is primarily an *aversion*. In an aversion addiction, the characteristic symptoms of addiction will simply appear as a mirror image. For instance, if withdrawal symptoms, a kind of stress reaction that occurs when addictive behavior is curtailed, are characteristically

---

[15] *Ibid.* p. 3

[16] *Ibid.* pp. 24-25.

found in an addiction of attraction, an aversion addiction will present *approach* symptoms, feelings of panic or fear when I get too close to what I wish to avoid.[17]

For May, the way to overcoming an addiction involves an interaction between will and grace, which he calls empowerment. "For the power of addiction to be overcome, human will must act in concert with divine will. The human spirit must flow with the Holy Spirit. Personal power must be aligned with the power of grace."[18] Empowerment sets us on a journey, a life process that has as its end what May identifies with conversion. He calls it *homecoming*.

> The journey homeward, the process of homemaking in God, involves withdrawal from addictive behaviors that have become normal for us. In withdrawal, attachments are lessened, and their energy is freed for simpler, purer desire and care. In other words, human desire is freed for love.[19]

I have used Gerald May's words extensively here for it seems to me that his treatment of addiction and grace are a timely articulation of what thousands of people are finding to be a practical and realistic way

---

[17] *Ibid.* pp. 36-37.

[18] *Ibid.* p. 140.

[19] *Ibid.* p. 95.

to pursue conversion. In Twelve-Step Programs around the country, tremendous strides in personal growth and freedom are taking place. And beyond the structures of formal Twelve-Step groups, many people are discovering through the exploration of patterns of co-dependency that there is a way to break out of addictive entrapment.

This says something very new about conversion, and yet it is not new at all. Conversion is to be a liberation, breaking the shackles of our own enslavement. The Gospel tells us that. We are in thrall to sin, mindlessly pursuing it as something we are inclined at times to call good, or desirable, or tolerable. Sin wears many masks; some of them are even socially acceptable, many offer us status, or power, or comfort. On occasion sinfulness even speaks in a religious language (as the devil did in the gospels). Conversion names what we must do to break out of our addictions of the human spirit.

Of course, this understanding of conversion asks us to broaden our theology of sin. In addictive patterns sin will not always be a matter of conscious choosing. I do not actively set about to *choose* an addiction; I am more likely to fall into one. Often I discover that conversion begins in the middle. I wake up to discover that I have become entwined in something. As we know from our experience, this kind of sin often appears as mindless behavior. The false self within us has been lulled into a trap. Perhaps it seemed in our best interest, but it has only served to keep us from our heart's desire.

But what of our understanding of sin as a conscious choice against God? Does this mean I am culpable for what I didn't even choose? Is that fair of God? It is worth noting that in the last 400 years the Church has been too fixated on culpability to begin with. This is very clear from the prevalence of what has come to be known as the "Catholic neurosis," *guilt.* There is much to say about the need to take responsibility for our actions, and real conversion, by the very nature of freedom, will *always* imply a conscious choice for God. Yet sinfulness is much broader than we have understood it. The most profound definition of sin is not "what I did wrong," but instead it is what keeps me from living out the Gospel call to discipleship, what blocks my relationship with God. This is *at least* as much true of our addictive behaviors as it is of a decision one Sunday morning to roll over in bed, thereby missing Mass.

It must also be evident that the addictive nature of sin goes far beyond the many ways we discover ourselves to be personally bound. It is true that we can look into the movement of our lives and discover all sorts of mindlessly debilitating dynamics -- greed, apathy, the desire for immediate gratification, the desire for success and recognition, manipulations, depersonalizations, and self-destructive patterns, to name a few. However, we must also be aware that all of these are not simply sins committed by isolated individuals. We are socially bound as well. Sinfulness can never totally be something that remains just between God and me. We must begin to explore the addictive nature of social sin as well. Injustice, militarism, power-seeking, consumerism, racial and ethnic bigotry, sexism, destruction of the environment, and so many others -- these so easily get under our communal skin, where they live and breed and fester. They too are most often mindless and addictive.

Into the midst of our growing awareness of the addictive nature of human sinfulness has emerged an ancient tool. The Enneagram, as I have studied it over the last dozen or so years, has presented itself to me as a valuable instrument for approaching just this view of our brokenness and bondage. Possibly the most beneficial aspect of the Enneagram is that it does not stop at giving us an accurate description of our addictive nature, but it goes on to offer concrete directional movement to enable us to better pursue conversion. We now turn directly to explore this potential tool for conversion spirituality.

THREE

THE ENNEAGRAM

THE STORY: THE DISCOVERED STONE

Once upon a time a traveler was journeying along a country road. As he walked along, his mind wandered from one thing to another, caught up as it was in all the important events of his life. When the road ended abruptly at the bank of a shallow stream, the man didn't hesitate for a second, because he saw that on the far bank the road took up again. Confidently he waded into the water. But he had gone only a third of the way through the stream when his foot hit upon something hard and rather large, causing him to lose his balance and stumble into the water. He came up unhurt, but very wet and angry. He groped around to see what he had tripped on, and found in the bed of the stream a large and beautiful stone. He had never seen anything like it. Somewhat rounded in shape, it seemed to sparkle from hundreds of unseen lights. This was, he concluded, a remarkable find, and not wanting to simply return the beautiful stone to the water, he decided that, even though it was heavy and awkward, he would take it with him on his journey.

That evening he came to an inn, and having procured a room he went to the common room to purchase a meal. There were many travelers at the inn, and the meal continued on while one after another they related the adventures of their respective journeys. As he was sharing the many hardships he had endured upon the road, he happened to mention his discovery of the stone, and having his knapsack with him, he removed the stone and showed it to all in the room. So engrossed was he in the story he was telling that he hardly took notice of the hush that fell over the room as all eyes fixed on the stone.

That night in his room with his knapsack safely tucked by his pillow -- for he was actually a cautious person -- he had almost drifted off to sleep when there burst into his room the dark shadow of a figure who immediately lunged for the knapsack. It took all the man's strength and indignation to drive the intruder off. Finally having done so, it occurred to him, of course, that it was the stone the thief had wanted. It was obviously more valuable than he had first supposed. He resolved to proceed as soon as possible into the nearby city and assess its worth.

After restlessly passing the remainder of the night, the man proceeded early the next morning toward the city, carefully guarding the stone, and went directly to the section of the city where the gem dealers managed their shops. Entering a shop that appeared well kept and prosperous, he presented the stone to the dealer. He noticed the man's eyes grow large as he carefully examined it. After what seemed to be an extraordinarily long period of time, the dealer put down his eye piece and said, "Sir, you have found a diamond... but not an ordinary diamond. This is indeed a truly valuable gem. I am a fair man, and would not cheat you, so I must tell you that the worth of this stone is beyond my capacity. I cannot relieve you of your find."

Elated to hear of the stone's worth, he still could not help feeling rather discouraged that he might not easily be able to relieve himself of what seemed to be a growing burden. The man began to look for another dealer, for it was a prosperous city. Surely there must be someone who would be able to purchase this diamond. Yet each dealer had a similar story; none would offer to take the gem from the traveler. Finally, at the very last shop the man could find, almost at the point of despair he cried out, asking if there was no one who would buy this stone.

"My friend," responded the dealer, "we gem dealers have limited resources, and you have not found an ordinary stone. There are no dealers here who will take it. However, I have heard that deep in the distant woods there is an old jewel dealer of a different sort. I myself have never met her, but perhaps she is one who might be interested in your diamond."

Feeling a glimmer of hope return, the man took his gem and began a day's journey into the forest. He came at last to a little cottage, hidden away in a dark corner of the woods. Connected to the cottage was a little shop with a few scattered gems visible to the customer. Behind a shabby little counter stood an old woman, bent over but sharp of eye and quick of mind. The man pulled the gem from his knapsack and, without a word, placed it on the counter before the woman. She glanced at it for the briefest moment.

"I see you have found one," she said. "You were wise to come here. What are you willing to pay for the jewel?"

"Pay? I don't want to *buy* this; I was trying to get rid of it. It is *I* who am trying to sell this diamond, which has weighed heavily on me since I found it."

"My friend," she said, "you have come a long way at great trouble, so I will be direct with you. You have found this diamond, but it is not yours. This diamond is not like others. It has the power to reveal great treasures... but only to the trained eye. If you purchase this diamond, your travels will be ended; if you relinquish it, any further travels will be to no avail. Its price is high. You must give up all else that you desire. In order to possess this kind of diamond, one must consent to live with the greatest of cost."

THE ROOTS OF THE ENNEAGRAM

One of the conclusions that I am suggesting is essential to an understanding of conversion is that it has something to do with personal and social liberation. A belief in this statement lays the groundwork for seeing the possibility that the Enneagram could be a tremendous aid in the conversion process. The reason is simple; if the Enneagram is about anything, it is about *freedom*.

Some people who have had a passing exposure to this system might be surprised at this statement. There are many whose encounter, not with the Enneagram but with people who have "studied" it, has led them to the conclusion that it is little more than a pop-psychology party game for people who sit around and put numbers on themselves and others. Perhaps they have themselves been assigned a number, and upon learning the description of that number, one through nine, have felt labeled, categorized, and, in short, anything but freed by the Enneagram. It would be an understandable reaction for such people to state emphatically that they will *never* pursue such things. It would be understandable; it would also be unfortunate, for the Enneagram, if it is about *anything*, is about freedom.

Our society clings to some strange illusions about freedom. We have, for instance, sometimes equated it with license. "I am free to do whatever I want, as long as no one gets hurt." (As if I could always know!) Or sometimes it is equated with option -- the ability to shop at K-mart, or Sears, or anywhere else I "choose." And it is sometimes equated with individual rights. As a result, we often find ourselves in a position where the good of our communal rights is held hostage by an isolated exemption. However we understand these "freedoms," they are not the kind of freedom offered by the Enneagram. A major focus of this chapter is the exploration of what sort of liberation this spiritual tool can present to us.

The Enneagram as a tool for freedom and transformation has gradually become known in contemporary Western culture throughout this century. It was first introduced to the West as a key piece in the teachings of George Ivanovich Gurdjieff in pre-Soviet Russia, and was brought to France by Gurdjieff when he fled the revolution. Gurdjieff claimed that it embodied the whole of human knowledge, and through it all knowledge could be interpreted.[1] The Enneagram, a nine-pointed figure (the basic meaning

---

[1] Ouspensky, Peter D. *In Search of the Miraculous.* New York and London: Harcourt Brace Jovanovich, 1977. p. 294.

of the Greek word) placed within a circle, was for Gurdjieff a symbol of perpetual motion and process, and represented the unfolding of the most fundamental laws of the universe. Following his death in 1949, various aspects of his teaching, including the Enneagram, were carried on by several of his students, most notably, Peter Ouspensky, John Bennett, and Maurice Nicoll. Gurdjieff's teaching on the Enneagram focused on the symbol as representing an unfolding process. In the 1970s Oscar Ichazo, a native of Bolivia, began offering a different approach to the Enneagram. In an institute he opened in Arica, Chile, Ichazo presented the symbol as a paradigm for understanding different aspects of human nature. Ichazo has since moved the Arica Institute to New York, where he still offers extensive training programs through his particular methodology. This basic understanding of the Enneagram, with additional variations, was presented by Claudio Naranjo, who learned this new approach from Ichazo, in programs offered at Esalen in California. Through Naranjo and others who studied it under him, this understanding of the Enneagram as a model for human transformation has since been widely disseminated.

Speculation has long existed concerning the sources for the information passed on by Gurdjieff and Ichazo. While their approaches are closely related, it is evident that the two received the material independently of each other. However, it is widely believed that behind the Gurdjieff and Ichazo material lies a common tradition. But what is this tradition? It is likely that its roots are lost for the most part in antiquity, buried in an oral tradition that some speculate even in part pre-dates the Christian era. It seems to have arisen within the Eurasian-Semitic world, and probably developed gradually over time as one religious and cultural influence superimposed itself upon another.

There are many spiritual hands that have influenced the molding of the Enneagram, and to be able to distill the various contributions would seem hopeless. Was there an influence of Zoroastrianism upon the system? What impact did Greek culture have (as evidenced in the very name of the symbol)? What was the contribution of the Judeo-Christian tradition? And were there any early Eastern influences? (Ichazo has cast the Enneagram in a more Eastern-occult mode, but it is not at all clear how long-standing an aspect of the tradition this really is.)

Most advocates of the Enneagram are in agreement at least that it was passed on in history primarily through the spiritual tradition known as Sufism. Sufism is a more mystical branch of Islam, and historically has manifested itself through the development of various strains referred to as *orders*, traditions analogous to the variations of Christian spirituality arising from the different forms of religious life. It is believed that within one of these orders, the Naqshbandi Order, the Enneagram was passed on under tightly controlled circumstances. There is conjecture of the existence of a group referred to as the Sarmouni Brotherhood, which at least might have been the source of a major part of Gurdjieff's information. There is, however, little of a concrete nature to go on.

What is clear is that Sufism has greatly influenced the spirituality and philosophy of the Enneagram.

In our post-Vatican II age of interfaith dialogue, this eclectic spiritual background has attracted many Christians, and there has been a growing interest in the Enneagram in various Church circles. That it seems to correlate so well with many contemporary psychological perspectives makes it all the more attractive. It has, however, been a source of concern among some fundamentalist Christians, who remain suspicious of its mysterious background. This is ironic since the Enneagram is probably much closer to the thought patterns of the Semitic world of the Scriptures than is the world view of Medieval Scholasticism.

Confusion has arisen in some quarters around the esoteric roots of the Enneagram, an esotericism that it seems to me primarily served the purpose of maintaining the purity of the system. There has been a superficial effort to link the Enneagram with the heresy of Gnosticism, because of the use Sufis make of pursuing *gnosis*, or knowledge, as a path to God. This reveals a lack of understanding of the Enneagram. Basic tenets of the Gnostic heretical doctrine -- such as the absolute separation of God from created matter; a total ontological dualism between matter and spirit; a view of the material world as inherently evil; the struggle of the human spirit to free itself from the evil world of matter; salvation through knowledge apart from divine assistance; and the presence of the extremes of severe asceticism and wreckless indulgence -- all inimical to the true Christian faith, also stand in direct opposition to human transformation as understood from the perspective of the Enneagram. In fact, this line of thinking also reveals some basic misunderstandings of essential Sufi belief. As Victor Danner states:

> Gnosis eventually became the preferred term in Sufism to describe the goal of the Path, although other terms are also used, likewise implying knowledge of the divine mysteries and realities. But it should not be confused with any special type of Gnosticism that existed in the early Christian Church -- being heretical in its teachings as well as heteroclite and syncretistic in its absorption of non-Christian elements, such Gnosticism was in stark contrast with the quite legitimate gnosis of the Greek Fathers and of the later Hesychasts. The *ma'rifah* of Sufism is not something occultist or bizarre; as understood by the Sufis, gnosis comes with ever-deepening faith, and not contrary to it or outside of it. Nor is it possible for anyone dispossessed of the fear or respect of the Divinity to reach that gnosis through a kind of backdoor to the Path, for there is none. Therefore, one should add to the concepts of love and knowledge that attach themselves to Sufi gnosis the notion of the reverential fear of God, which breeds a distrust of the world

as other-than-God, and prepares the way
for the love and knowledge of the Real.[2]

In the final analysis, speculative as it is due to
our lack of substantial data, we must conclude that the
strongest spiritual influences on the Enneagram
system have been through the Western spiritual
tradition (the Judeo-Christian-Islamic line). Still the
Enneagram, as it comes to us today, cannot be understood as a Christian tool. This is far different, however, from concluding that it stands at odds with the
Christian tradition. As it has come to us, the Enneagram is a non-doctrinal spirituality. It does not seek to
use the theological language of any spiritual tradition,
but chooses to approach the Divine first through
universal human experience.

What does this mean for the Christian who
comes to encounter this system? Like every other
aspect of life presented to us today, the Enneagram
must be discerned and evaluated based on how well
it helps us to fulfill the Christian project, that is, the
living out of the Gospel of Jesus Christ, and our
cooperation with the unfolding Reign of God that the
Gospel heralds. We have spoken of the two sources
of revealed faith, the Scriptures and the Apostolic
Tradition. If the Enneagram is to be seen as a
powerful tool in our process of conversion, we need

---

[2] Danner, Victor. Introduction to *Ibn Ata'illah.
The Book of Wisdom*, (The Classics of Western
Spirituality series). New York: Paulist Press, 1978. pp.
12-13.

not look for the use of a stock religious language, but we must find its fruitfulness to be in keeping with what we as Christians accept as revealed truth. To properly evaluate this, it is necessary to seek a separation of the Enneagram as a non-doctrinal tool of spirituality from the many contemporary voices who would seek to give it their own particular bent.

THE MANY FACES OF THE ENNEAGRAM

In the years that I have been using the Enneagram as a personal tool for conversion in my life, as well as in the use I have made of it in spiritual ministry, I have found that it offers us potential benefits as both a *model* and a *process*. As a *model* the Enneagram has attracted a great deal of attention in recent years. It is easy to find workshops, retreats, and seminars offering to train people on various levels of its use. Books and tapes have been published both introducing the system and expanding upon it in humanistic and spiritual ways. On the Enneagram as a *process* much less seems to be available, and much of that is not easily accessible to the average person.

In its form as a model the Enneagram can represent many things, since it is constructed around universal laws of creation, but most often it has come to be identified with various aspects of what people call "personality." This is a problematic term since there is no real agreement on just what this word means. Is it something vital and essential to our lives, or does it correlate with what Ernest Becker called *character*, which he referred to as our "vital lie?"[3] The question of personality speaks to our ongoing problem with the limits of language when referring to our own mysterious being. This problem is not always aided by attempting to create another more specific language, which often only complicates matters even further.

Models and paradigms are popular in both psychology and religion. We have, for instance, models of behavioral style, developmental models, models of Church, and prayer, and liturgy, and so on. One good example of the use of models, where psychology and religion have tended to overlap in their application, is in the Myers-Briggs Type Indicator, abbreviated MBTI,[4] which was developed as a behavioral preference instrument from a Jungian personality theory of human attitudes and functions. It has been successfully adapted in many ways by business, Church, and educational groups into a very useful tool.

Part of the contemporary appeal of models is that they fit so well into our pluralistic experience of life. They enable us to approach some very complex realities and understand them better without reducing

---

[3] Becker, Ernest. *The Denial of Death*. New York: Free Press, Macmillan Publishing Co., 1973. p. 56.

[4] Myers, Isabel Briggs. *The Myers-Briggs Type Indicator, Manual (1962)*. Palo Alto, CA: Consulting Psychologists Press, Inc., 1962.

them to one-dimensional constructions. Models also allow us the awareness that people see things in different ways. Such models are, however, essentially cognitive. They are educational constructions that help us better understand intellectually various aspects of a certain reality. While they are helpful, they are also limited. Intellectual understanding, as helpful as it is, is only one aspect of complete knowledge.

The Enneagram certainly is a model, in fact a very precise and complex model. It is, however, more than that. Many people have been introduced to it as a "self-knowledge" system. It is this. However, if we expect this knowledge to be merely intellectual we will unduly limit the Enneagram's potential. It is also meant to be an experiential tool, one that opens us more completely to the processes of our lives, one that offers us a way, not simply of understanding human transformation, but also of helping us to *enter into* the process of transformation.

In its tradition the Enneagram has most frequently been transmitted through this language of human transformation. It implies some kind of a change, a change not just of appearance but of substantial nature. Throughout this book I have used the language of conversion. It too is understood as dealing with substantial change, change toward a positive spiritual and religious life project. Conversion is a language of religious structure. Transformation is a language that some non-doctrinal circles feel more comfortable with. Yet in the experiential the two processes coincide. It is conceivable that conversion and transformation might to some extent have different points of focus, yet experientially individuals who are on the life journey are asked to move in a direction that gives meaning to both languages.

In utilizing either the language of transformation or of conversion we must still affirm a basic premise. As a tool for the life journey the Enneagram must be experiential. Its fruitfulness as a means of leading people closer to God and more in touch with their true selves will ultimately not be what it teaches them *about* themselves, although of course this is not inconsequential. Its fruit will lie in how well it leads them beyond themselves to encounter the greater forces of life and the very mystery of God.

This presumes a faith stance and a rootedness in a tradition. Saints and spiritual writers of all religious backgrounds point to the need for such rootedness. I would urge all people using the Enneagram for conversion and transformation to have or be seeking a tradition. It will be obvious to readers that I approach and understand the Enneagram from within a Christian faith stance. This book could not have been written were that not the case. The Enneagram as a non-doctrinal tool, however, allows for many approaches. It must be recognized that it has been presented from several spiritual viewpoints.

The Gurdjieff tradition was the first to introduce the Enneagram as a tool for transformation. George Ivanovich Gurdjieff (1870's - 1949) was thought by many to be an extraordinary teacher and master of the spiritual life. He was also a controversial figure whose unusual manner and techniques have been criticized, and leave him an enigma even to many who highly respect his teaching. Many of the principles of the Gurdjieff "Work," as Gurdjieff referred to the process of transformation, are of utmost help in the conversion process. Some of the teachings of the Work are obscure at best and even of questionable value in the long run.[5] Gurdjieff was interested in conscious living, in bringing humanity out of its state of sleep, or life experienced only at an automatic or mechanical level. Gurdjieff claimed that we are *machines*. Much of what we do, even much of what seems to us to be our "free choices," arises from a life of highly conditioned responses. The first task of transformation is to recognize this level of unconsciousness. Gurdjieff taught many techniques and exercises to enable people to break out of their patterned existence.

The Enneagram is not simply one of these techniques. It is instead the paradigm that gives form to all of them. Gurdjieff taught that it is a symbolic expression of universal laws; first, the Law of Trinity, which he believed to be the fundamental law of creation, and second, the Law of Octaves, representing the structure of how creation is ordered. The continuous interacting of these laws and the complex unfolding of the Enneagram's nine points in relationship to one another held the secrets, according to Gurdjieff, of how the universe functioned.

---

[5] While many of the writings of Gurdjieff are published, their complicated nature often discourages the prospective student. Many people learn of Gurdjieff through the writings of others. Refer to the Suggested Reading List at the end of this book for some possible places to start.

While certainly a gifted individual, Gurdjieff had an eccentric personality, and his efforts have been criticized because his life did not always seem to be congruent with his teachings. Moreover, Gurdjieff was very secretive about his knowledge. He discouraged dilittantism, the mere cursory exploration of his ideas, and purposely made his lectures complex and obscure. Nor did he single out any of his primary disciples as the named successors of the tradition. We find at present that the body of his teaching has been somewhat factionalized by many different "schools" of the Gurdjieff Work. Kathleen Riordan Speeth, for instance, lists no less than 11 different lines of transmission of the Work at present.[6]

Gurdjieff did not clearly develop the Enneagram as a model of the variations within human nature. He made references to an individual's "chief fault," but did not seem to elaborate on this.[7] Some have raised the question of whether this was in fact a part of the tradition of his teachers that he had not completely mastered.

Oscar Ichazo, the founder of the Arica Institute, seems to have been the first to publicly correlate different aspects of human nature with the nine points

---

[6] Speeth, Kathleen Riordan. *The Gurdjieff Work.* New York: Pocket Books, Simon & Schuster, 1976. p. 151.

[7] See, for instance, Ouspensky, P.D. *In Search of the Miraculous.* New York and London: Harcourt Brace Jovanovich, 1977. p. 226.

of the Enneagram. In the early 1970s, through the instructions of Ichazo's Arica Institute, and subsequently through other sources like Claudio Naranjo and John Lilly, who had various connections with it, variations of this nine-pointed model began to spread, particularly through what is generally known as the "human potential movement." While the essential idea under the various configurations of the Enneagram is the same, the specific forms that each has taken reflect the particular interest and spiritual view of each of the transmitters.

The Arica Institute has developed the Enneagram along more non-Western lines, showing a high influence from Zen and other Eastern traditions. Ichazo has chosen to keep his material more esoteric, and has been rather protective of his system and its use by other people. One result of this has been less of a dependence on Ichazo's form, and a greater emphasis by other authors on their own individual exploration of the ideas that lie beneath a specific format. The system, therefore has come to be transmitted in a variety of forms, so that no particular language is proving to be the definitive version. This has left people who wish to utilize the Enneagram as a tool for transformation in a position of needing to continuously seek the reality that lies behind the various language forms. While many may feel frustrated by this, it is actually in some way an advantage, since the mystery of our spiritual journey can never be totally contained in a language.

Claudio Naranjo, who learned of the identification of the nine points on the Enneagram from Ichazo while the latter was still in Chile, has also influenced the tradition in two ways. First, he has adapted the model to embrace the contemporary psychological language professionally understood in this country. Second, his transmission of the material has been widely disseminated through two of his own students, Robert Ochs and Helen Palmer, who both reside in the San Francisco Bay area. Ochs' transmission of the Enneagram material through his teaching was the initial training received by many who have made the Enneagram available to a wider audience. His influence has continued to be felt through a number of printed and taped works that have appeared in recent years.[8]   Palmer, herself a recent author on the Enneagram, has added to the tradition through her own understanding of individual intuitive styles and the first-hand interviewing of representative persons in the various Enneagram life positions.

While all the contemporary works on the Enneagram have substantial differences, it is safe to say that they have much more in common. All express an understanding of nine basic modes of human living,

---

[8]   Many of the current books and tapes that present or refer to the Enneagram as a model of nine variations of human nature, including this one, have been directly or indirectly influenced by Robert Ochs. I am indebted to him for introducing me to the Enneagram through courses I took with him in the late 1970s. Rather than make a partial list of other works that come from this source, I again refer the reader to the Suggested Reading List at the end of this book.

often named through different expressions. Each mode is initially expressed and recognized through a variety of negative behavioral patterns, which manifest a basic character or personality flaw. While the current literature represents these primarily through behavioral characteristics and patterns of life, I would like to suggest that they are pointing to a much deeper core, a fundamental flaw in motivations.

Each mode of living, however, is also potentially transformable, and, as the literature suggests, moves in some way to a positive construction. Most of the literature presumes the gradual appearance of an unfolding essential nature, an original grace, or a spiritual destiny. It is my basic assertion throughout this book that this movement of life toward our essential nature, our true self, or what Jesus speaks of as the life one saves in entering discipleship, is the movement of conversion identified in the Gospel.

Many readers, no doubt, are familiar with the Enneagram model. I urge those who are not to explore the model through individual instruction, workshops, or courses. If necessary, familiarization with the model at least through books and tapes would be an aid in exploring conversion. As I stated in the Introduction, this book presumes a basic under-standing of the Enneagram model. For the most part I would like to concentrate on the Enneagram as a *process*, and direct my comments to presenting this spiritual tool in the context of a Christian theology of conversion.

THE ENNEAGRAM IN A CONVERSION SPIRITUALITY

As conversion does, our use of the Enneagram begins in the *middle*. In the middle of my life, in the midst of my daily routine, my ordinary comings and goings, I become aware of a core set of life responses. I experience them as patterned behaviors or unconsciously repeated actions and expressions that I never before took the time to reflect upon. When I do, I sense that these patterns have been there as long as I can remember. While they might have been nuanced in various ways over the years, I now sense an eerily consistent core.

I discover these patterns in different ways. Sometimes they are recognized in feedback I receive from other people. In general, people tell me the truth. It often comes with their own baggage, expectations and assumptions they place upon me, often unfairly. Yet when I separate other's baggage from their feedback, often there is the truth, sometimes too stark and frightening to deal with. It is easier to blame them or justify myself, but then, grace abounds, and sometimes I allow their truth-telling to settle on me.

Often I discover the patterns of my life through my own self-observations. One day I am doing something or saying something, and I am subtly aware that I have done or said this kind of thing before. I am aware that I didn't choose to do it; I didn't even think about it. I just did it, as I have in the past, perhaps as I have done many times in the past. Often these patterns are recognized through negative emotion, shaded aspects of anger, fear, depression, apathy, anxiety, or a free-floating feeling that something is just not right. Sometimes I might even experience these patterns connected with what I have identified as a gift or talent. The only problem is that here in the middle of my life I am painfully aware that I have not *chosen* any of it.

The presence of negative emotion is an important clue. When I begin to explore the experience or pattern more deeply, I discover this negative feeling is just the tip of the iceberg. I find that this experience is subtly connected to a whole complex of experiences that have manifested themselves as truly painful in the course of my life. I slowly become aware of how pervasive this pattern has been. This experience, linked with so many others, begins to reveal itself as something that is frustrating the deepest desire for that spiritual oneness at the heart of my quest for God.

As the process of my life continues, my awareness begins to grow. I begin to find common threads, ways in which one experience links to another. I discover that what I do in the work arena is essentially just a variation of what I do at home. Or to my surprise and bewilderment, I discover they are opposite. I also increasingly discover that I am powerless to stop these forms of behavior. When I make a concerted effort to control them, I become angry, frustrated, stressed, and often my efforts end in failure. I am also gradually aware that I do not know *why* I do these things. They are at some level unexplainable, and that is all the more frustrating.

Every one of us has gone through and will go through this process. If I say I have not, I can take no pride in this, for it means my life has remained basically at a level of unawareness. The above description, as uncomfortable and distressing as it might be, is actually citing an activity of grace, for it is asking me to test the very motivational structure of the responses I make to life.

The Enneagram offers us a spectrum of core motivational responses. I might, for instance, be driven by a passion to experience the good things of life. Shying away from what the ego perceives as painful or problematic, I seek endless options of pleasurable experiences, fruitlessly seeking to prove myself on top of life. The Enneagram places this motivational core in the SEVEN position. In classical spirituality it has pointed to a fundamental distortion of life known as Gluttony.

Or, as another example, I might be motivated toward various forms of inertia. Lacking a true sense of self, I seek to find a substitute in creating an environment that is comfortable to me, one that offers no internal conflicts. I might do this by busying myself with frenetic energy in mindless projects, or I might simply do nothing. In the meantime the things that truly need to be done in life are left unattended. Classical spirituality has referred to this lack of essential activity as Sloth. The Enneagram positions this motivational core in the NINE space.

The Enneagram offers seven other motivational responses, all symbolically fitted in the nine life positions on its circular configuration. It is not that the Enneagram is basically negative; quite the contrary. The essential nature of the Enneagram is transforming. It is, however, first experienced sequentially as negative. In a conversion spirituality this should not surprise us. Jesus first appears preaching repentance, a return to what we were made for, away from something we have fallen into.

As I become more aware of my behavioral patterns and more able to identify them as related to one of these motivational cores, I discover that I am facing some long standing aspects of my life. They can often be traced to my childhood, to the ways in which I responded to significant early experiences in my life. I begin to question myself: Have I been doing similar things my whole life? Has so much of my activity come from this common motivational set of responses? Is it possible that even apparently opposite behavior could be motivated from the same source?

This last query is not, after all, so strange. Someone in the motivational position of the ONE space, for instance, who has the need to structure her experience of reality around pre-conceived mental patterns, often finds herself becoming angry and possibly enraged when the circumstances don't match the pattern. Yet this same person carries around another pre-conceived mental image that believes anger is bad or evil. So unconsciously she places a mental construction in her mind that triggers a friendly, happy response to what irritates her. Psychology calls this *reaction formation*; her friends experience it as something that makes her overly gushy, and not in touch with her true feelings; she sees it as just trying to be good.

The Enneagram theorizes that each of us is coming from one of the nine motivational life positions. This core motivation does not change, nor would it be any advantage to us if it could, since all the fundamental life positions have their flawed and distorted aspects. All of them, of course, also have their transforming qualities. Each one offers us a response to grace; each one asks us to produce certain fruits worthy of conversion.

But where did the motivational core come from? Did I learn it? Did I pick it up from my early life experiences? Was I born with it? Could it be inherited? Is it a combination of all of these? While these are excellent questions (questions asked at almost every workshop I have given on the Enneagram), in the context of conversion they are of secondary concern.[9] We can at least say that my early environment greatly modified and formed the particular manifestation of my life position. Yet conversion primarily asks me to deal with what I find in my life, and not to get lost in speculation over where it came

---

[9] The answer to this line of questioning, as I perceive it, is still open. People who emphasize a strictly psychological approach to the Enneagram tend to favor an environmental cause as the source of one's life position. It is, however, a preconception on the part of most psychological schools that our primary adult work is the resolving of our unresolved childhood issues. While this might generally be true, I am not sure that we can make absolute such a simplified presumption in regard to essential nature.

from. Certainly, by the time I discover my motivational core it has already been rooted in me for a long time. It is that locked-in quality that calls forth action from me. Mere speculation of origin will never be sufficient to bring about substantial change.

The identification of this fundamental life position is an important first step in using the Enneagram as a tool for conversion. In the process of this self-identification two other factors come into my awareness as well. The first is *self-deception*, and the second is *resistance*. When I recognize my fundamental life pattern, I also recognize that these two factors have been present for a long time.

The Enneagram, by its nature, is involved in the search for truth, and that truth begins with some admissions about my own life. I suddenly become so much more aware of what I have hidden from myself. It is not that I have been consciously pretending to be what I am not, not that I have been trying to lie to others in an overt way. Most often it is that I have tended to focus on my best motives and unconsciously conceal aspects of many others. My self-deception is cloaked in partial truth, the most difficult deception to name. I speak to groups of the need to employ Holy Suspicion, an unrecognized virtue. I mean that we need to suspect our motives, and discern the whole truth of what we intend by our words and actions.

The other factor that comes to light with self-identification is resistance. This is an automatic tendency within us to block and frustrate a positive growth process. It is the height of our own human "craziness" that we tend to sabotage the things we most need and want. Psychologists speak of "secondary gains," the tendency to settle for hidden "payoffs" that do us no real good and only keep real maturity at a distance. Through a variety of defense mechanisms we can keep the recognition of our life position on the Enneagram away from us indefinitely. Moreover, even following recognition our resistance can block concrete action that we might have fruitfully chosen to take in regard to conversion.

One common manifestation of resistance often present with our initial encounter of the Enneagram could be called *misidentification*. This is when I name myself as centered in one Enneagram life position when in fact I am motivated by another. There are innocent reasons why I might misidentify. The various motivational languages are often very close, and frequently can seek to explain commonly held behavioral patterns. Someone in the TWO space, for instance, might be intent on reaching out to others and helping strangers in order to win approval and be recognized as warm and friendly. Someone in the SIX space might do something very similar for a very similar reason. The TWO is fulfilling his image of himself as a lovable, giving person. The SIX could be trying to embody an internalized message of how she is *expected* to act. These two motivational drives look and sound very close when met in real life. While a reaction of Pride seems like it would look very different from one of Fear, it is not always so in the concrete.

Misidentification, however, is not always nearly so innocent. In Jungian psychology what is referred to as the *Shadow*, the unrecognized and often unwanted parts of myself, is projected, repressed, and denied by the conscious self. Many of these shadow elements are present in my Enneagram life position. My resistance to owning them can be so strong that I might unconsciously "disown" them by choosing another position that generally fits me behaviorally but does not truly name my core. I might be very resentful that someone would suggest I consider another space. I might present all kinds of reasons why this suggestion could not possibly be true. Again, an exercise in Holy Suspicion could help to go a long way in fruitfully overcoming this resistance.

I have stated that the identification of my life position on the Enneagram is an important step in using it as a tool for conversion. This does not mean, however, that it is a *big* step. Actually, in the recognition of my life position nothing has really changed at all; I haven't yet converted anything. This recognition is important, not in itself, but in what it now enables me to do. I now have the potential for *choice*. While I was unaware of my behaviors and their motivations, conscious change was not yet possible. Real change, real conversion, always requires conscious action.

To the extent that I am bound up in life patterns I never recognize, and motivations I cannot admit to, the ego, or false self, continues to act blindly in ways that are self-destructive, and in turn harmful to others. Being unaware, I am also unfree, held in thrall to mindless actions and motives that continuously frustrate my peace, drag me into manipulation and violence, and block my deepest desire to be at one with God.

With real awareness comes real choice, a great gift of grace. With the possibility of choice lies the potential for freedom. A liberation of spirit is offered to me. I have said that conversion can be recognized in terms of liberation, but conversion also implies the turning from sin. We must examine more completely how this motivational core named by the Enneagram can be considered sinful.

THE ADDICTIVE NATURE OF THE MIND

On those occasions when we are truly honest with ourselves, our moments of Holy Suspicion, we can admit that many of the things we do each day, many of the reactive comments we make, many of the conclusions we arrive at, far from being based on real personal choices, look much more like automatic responses. Someone says something and I find myself commenting on it as I have in hundreds of similar situations. Or I walk into a new group of people and I find myself acting in the same way I always do with people I do not know. When Gurdjieff says that we are machines, he is referring to this type of behavior. To be called a machine is shocking, and we become resentful. Yet, we also know that we cannot totally dismiss the charge, because through much of our daily lives we sense that events are passing us by. To say that we are machines is to say something about *conditioning.*

Conditioning begins in our lives as soon as we come into the world. Even before we can clearly differentiate words, we learn to pick up inflections of voice and senses of touch that tell each of us that we have done well or that we are disapproved of. Through our early family upbringing, through our school years and the early years of socializing, we are at first subtly, and then more and more systematically, told how to act, what to think, how to feel, and even how to express those feelings.

Conditioning, it should be recognized, is not by any means all bad. It is at one level helpful, and even necessary. In many ways it allows us to conserve our personal energy by enabling us to develop habits and life patterns that do not require extensive decision making. Conditioning helps us to relate to others, to share a common ground of meaning and understanding. It lies at the heart of culture, which in turn is linked to art and technical advancement. In adverse circumstances conditioning helps us to survive, in that it is crucial in a process of adaptation. Without an openness to conditioning, it is hard to imagine what human life would look like, if in fact we could have survived as a species at all.

However, conditioning also has a down side. As we live our daily lives, there is a point where it ceases to be helpful and actually begins to be, first, a burden, and then actually detrimental to our holistic growth. As we grow from infancy we are conditioned to what is "normal." What we discover, however, is that this is simply a statement of what most people do. One of the deepest drives that we have is our desire to be *included*, to belong or to be accepted by others. There are good reasons, for instance, why in a tightly controlled culture "shunning" is one of the most effective means of discipline. From primitive society on, we have found creative ways of withholding our approval from individuals in order to force them to comply with the common position. Only the minority of these ways actually deal with overt physical force.

Our sense of belonging is given to each of us through a process called *enculturation,* an intricate system whereby we are conditioned to our group's norms. Each of us was brought up in an environment where we were presented with parental expectations, family messages, and tribal or ethnic traditions. There were things we were taught to do and not to do. We received a spectrum of beliefs, values, social customs, and group prejudices that are "givens" in our cultural milieu. Even if at some point I react to them and do the opposite, they still could well be directing my behavior and thought process.

While my conditioning is uniquely mine, the complex product given me by parents, family, school, church, etc., and projected onto my individual experiences, this conditioning still depends upon the total reinforcement of my society. If I am to belong to it, my society must agree to what is "good and proper" behavior on my part.[10] Charles Tart has referred to

---

[10] Again, language is a limited servant in this regard. So it is not the words that matter so much as it is the meaning behind the words. In some parts of our society, for instance, the word *bad* has come to mean good, arising from the culture of the streets. But it does not matter what word is used. Inner city youths are as much conditioned to be "bad" as an older generation has been conditioned to be "good." Both segments of the population are most often merely seeking peer approval.

the commonly held system of social norms and expectations by a given culture as *consensus trance.*[11] His choice of words here implies that social conditioning generally takes on the nature of a hypnotic state, one in which not only I but the entire society in which I live has taken on a state of sleep. My culture is able to survive this trance-like state, and I as an individual am able to function within it (usually quite easily), but spiritually we all pay a costly price.

> Consensus trance involves a loss of much of our essential vitality. It is (all too much) a state of partly suspended animation and inability to function, a daze, a stupor. It is also a state of profound abstraction, a great retreat from immediate sensory/instinctual reality to abstractions about reality.[12]

Tart characterizes the process whereby I come to a complete enculturation as a power relationship between the culture, the "hypnotizing" agent, and the individual, the "subject" of the trance. However, instead of the hour or so of a normal hypnotizing session, the individual is subjected to hypnotic suggestion for years, indeed through the course of a whole lifetime. This is reinforced through a process of

---

[11] Tart, Charles. *Waking Up: Overcoming the Obstacles To Human Potential.* Boston: New Science Library, Shambhala, 1986. pp. 85-106.

[12] *Ibid.* p. 85.

rewards and punishments. The individual is rewarded through affirmation and validation, and punished sometimes through physical force, and sometimes through various psychological and emotional forces, such as guilt and shame. These are all designed to reinforce the need for a conformity to the expected social standards.[13]

The power that underlies our acceptance of this state of *consensus trance*, it seems to me, is recognized when we become aware of the extent to which we simply presume it as "the way things are." We seldom question our culture. From the kinds of foods we eat to the grave duties we must perform, there is little pause to reflect upon them objectively. At earlier periods in history, when cultures were more or less isolated from each other, an individual could lead his or her whole life without ever seriously challenging cultural parameters. In the global village of our present experience it is less likely that cultural differences will not impact upon us. Yet, we are still badly shaken when our deeply held assumptions are shattered by the awakening from consensus trance. The Vietnam experience can show us, for instance, the widespread trauma produced when a sizable portion of the population begins to question a society's pre-established assumptions. Our experience *since* Vietnam, however, also reveals how easy it is to slip back into the "givens" of cultural conditioning.

To the extent that I am conditioned I am not free. Cultural conditioning at first can seem innocent

---

[13] *Ibid.* pp. 90-95.

enough. People from Alabama like grits, and Pennsylvanians love scrapple, and who is hurt in the process? Yet despite the innocent aspects of conditioning, despite even the rich variants that culture has produced, conditioning in many ways holds each of us bound. The reason for this is that in the state of our "fallen nature," in the presence of my false self, conditioning has gone wild. I have not just become conditioned to various foods and styles of clothing. I have also become locked into many things that ego uses to gratify itself and manipulate others.

My desire to belong drives me to do things that in the long run become very self-destructive. I am driven to success, for instance, sometimes at any price. To be a good person I must be on top, I tell myself. That is what my parents wanted. That is why they praised me so when I brought home A's on my report card; that is why I felt I had to excel in sports or forensics; that is why I became so competitive. I know that no one will stand in my way, because I know I have what it takes. I can win. I know I have to.

Or perhaps my need to belong drives me to protect myself. I was never sure what my family was trying to tell me; I couldn't read my teachers. I seemed to disappoint so many people. I wanted to belong, but it seemed that I couldn't. So I've come to think that I really didn't care. It's no wonder I became so suspicious of others, no wonder I still withdraw from them. I've found my niche and people who understand me. To hell with the rest of them. They're only out to get something from me anyhow. I need to look out for myself.

These two common aspects of ego-enlargement and ego-protection offer hundreds of variations. What is alarming is not so much that we think this way as the extent to which we think this way without even recognizing it. It would be one thing if I went out one day with the express purpose of overcoming everyone I met. The problem is that most of the time I don't think I'm doing that, even the times when I actually am. This is where some of my motives remain truly hidden, and where I remain unfree.

This kind of bondage ultimately blocks my life in God's Spirit. I am not called to self-enlargement, nor am I called to self-protection. I am called to discipleship, to living for the Reign of God. To do that there are certain things that must be present in my life. I am, for instance, called to a non-manipulative love. I am asked to seek a true faith upon which my discipleship will be based. I am called to an essential trust in life, trust in God, and trust in self and others. This is not naivete, but an essential recognition of life's goodness, of its nature as gift. I am asked to seek out relationship in community, justice in the face of life's limitations, and compassion in dealing with myself and others. All these experiences, and so many others, do not allow for conditioning. They are all *free responses*; ultimately they can *only* be free responses.

As we have seen, the Enneagram posits that each of us possesses a core set of distorted motivational life responses. This motivational core is first experienced by each of us as a variety of unconscious, or at least unfocused, conditioned patterns of behavior. As such, this core does not represent motivational actions based on free conscious decisions or moral choices, but it manifests a distortion of reality, a perspective on life gone haywire. Proponents of the Enneagram have used different words to articulate different aspects of this core. It has been called a fixation, a compulsion, a passion, a fundamental sin, and so forth. The language used is not nearly as significant as the ability to recognize it and take action to counter it.

The primary life distortion is much more pervasive than we would like to admit. It is, if you will, analogous to a gaseous substance that permeates the very atmosphere around us. There is not an aspect of our lives that is left untouched. Sometimes it takes on a very innocent appearance, looking like one of the hundreds of little "personality quirks" that cause us to say, "Oh, well, that's just me. People are always telling me I do that." Sometimes, however, the effects of my distorted nature are anything but innocent. Sometimes the actions that I take and the patterns that I lock myself into are grossly destructive of self. They withhold true peace and happiness from me; they keep me from pursuing holiness. Sometimes these patterns are very detrimental to my relationships, being ways in which I manipulate and cause pain to others. Often they are out of focus. I do not easily recognize them, or I rationalize them away or refuse to see their debilitating effects in my life.

This motivational core serves a "purpose" in our lives. Once when we were younger it acted as a set of responses that helped to defend us from a world that seemed so large and overwhelming. Then we thought we needed survival techniques to help us make it through. But in our adult lives this core has become so refined and developed that it no longer defends us. It has come in some way to *own* us. The ego, our false self, uses it now to protect itself from the perceived dangers of the world or as a means of self-enlargement, as a willful and arrogant pride.

As it manifests itself this primary life distortion, as I have said, in some way possesses me. The ego is not free to turn it on or off, to remain in its sway or move out from under it. In my false self I am bound to it, and it presents itself essentially as an addictive attachment. We have seen that an addiction is a compulsive behavior that limits or destroys our freedom, but the various addictions that we fall prey to do not always sit upon the behavioral surface. Addictions, whether addictions of attachment or aversion, seep into the layers of our lives. They get into our motivational perspectives. They attach to whatever offers itself as a foothold. If this is true of any addiction, it is all the more true of this fundamental life distortion the Enneagram describes. In fact, we could call this motivational core of the false self our *fundamental addiction*, because it is so deeply rooted, and because it potentially affects every aspect of our lives.

Gerald May names and explores five essential characteristics that make a true addiction:[14]   1) tolerance, 2) withdrawal symptoms, 3) self-deception, 4) loss of willpower, and 5) distortion of attention. In its addictive nature the ego's motivational core gives

---

[14] May, *op. cit.*, pp. 26-31.

evidence at an alarmingly deep level of all these characteristics.

Throughout our lives there has been an insidious growth and sophistication of our core life distortion. When we were young the ego's responses to life were relatively simple and basic, characteristic ways we dealt with family and early social relationships. In adolescence life became much more complex and the ego felt it needed greater differentiation and nuance to cope with the increasing demands of adulthood. With each new experience the ego is tempted to find newer ways of dealing with unexpected threat. We call this characteristic *tolerance*, the phenomenon whereby we need more of a substance to maintain the level of addiction. Our natural ability to adapt plays into the need we have to satisfy a growing tolerance, and we can find individuals who have become deeply entrenched in some highly sophisticated yet painfully harmful patterns.

In our life distortions we come under the sway of a dreadful illusion. Consciously or unconsciously the ego begins to tell itself that it cannot possibly hope to survive without its conditioned behavioral structures. This seems to bear itself out on those occasions when we try to do something different. Often we will experience these different modes of behavior as feeling "unnatural." We might feel odd, exposed, vulnerable. We scurry back to the safe ground of ego structure. In the process we have experienced what is called in the language of addictive behavior *withdrawal*. The stress of living outside our conditioned patterns seems too great. The aversion we have to what in an illusory way seems like death makes us cling all the more to what we have come to know, to what we have become accustomed to.

The third characteristic of an addiction, *self-deception*, is perhaps the most clearly observable from the point of view of the Enneagram. What we gain from our primary life distortion is nothing less than a delusional reinforcement of ego, the false self. It allows us to live in a fantasy world that only vaguely resembles reality. Just as easily as the alcoholic can create a world of denial, projection, and so on, finding intricate ways of avoiding facing the truth about the behavior that is apparent to all, so too each of us does the same kind of thing in a much less focused way around the accumulated images we have of ourselves. That it relates to such a wide range of our behaviors and so permeates our life responses makes it so much the harder to see. In calling for Holy Suspicion, the Enneagram urges each of us to break out of the bonds of our self-deceptions.

The implications of these addictive characteristics within our ego structure should be very clear. To the extent that each of us is operating out of this fundamental distortion of ego, we are not free to make the necessary life choices that ultimately are a response to grace. We are bound to our conditioning. We are bound to our attachments. We have a radical, if subtle, *loss of willpower.* I started out this chapter by saying that the Enneagram, if it is about anything, is about freedom, for I am not free where I have no will. The Enneagram offers each of us a tool that can be used to cooperate with the grace that God gives to lead us to claim our promised liberation.

Yet even the loss of the power of our will does not tell the whole story of the addictive nature of this primary trap of the ego. What we finally discover when we honestly search out the results of our trying to live out of ego's primary distortion is that it has caused each of us to center our desires on ourselves. We make the ultimate importance of our lives the image of our own egos. Gerald May is correct in naming this *distortion of attention* as an idolatry: "No matter how religious we may think we are, our addictions are always capable of usurping our concern for God."[15] The basis for understanding our distorted motivational core as sinful is the very same basis on which the Judeo-Christian-Islamic tradition has always placed its understanding of sin, that is, that every manifestation of sinfulness is in some way the worshipping of an idol. The greatest and most powerful idol we will place before God is our own false self. The greatest grace that God offers is the grace that allows us to once more focus our attention on the one who has called us into being.

We do not usually choose our addictions, in the sense of making conscious actions of will based on the recognition of free alternatives. Nor have we made an ultimate choice concerning the distorted motivational core that ego lives in. Yet this core distortion continues to affect the apparent choices we make every day. For instance, if I am a FIVE, with a motivational core that seeks to withhold myself, my emotions, and my truest thoughts through a stance of

---

[15] May, *op. cit.* p. 29.

observing my experiences rather than participating in them, I might think that I have freely chosen to pursue a career as a scientist, a theologian, or some other intellectual. However, I might have simply allowed ego to choose the path of least resistance. I might be unavailable to others so that I can pursue "important" things. While doing something that gains me respect, I might simply be continuing in activity that keeps me from entering into life and blocks the call of grace.

To the extent that our lives are ruled by these fundamental addictions named in the Enneagram we will continuously find our way blocked in all our attempts to seek Gospel discipleship. Even doing "good things" can actually be a hindrance if all they succeed in doing is to feed the false self, as Jesus tried to demonstrate to the Pharisees time and again. If we were to call this fundamental addiction our "original sin," it might have to be understood a bit differently from what Augustine spoke of, but it would be true to the nature of what he had in mind. It is something that we have all "fallen into," and it is something that we were freed from in the redemption of Jesus. However, it is of the very nature of this redemptive grace that we must be free to respond to it. If I am to be a "wise steward," one who takes the moment's initiative of grace, I must *act* toward the liberation that Christ offers. To be a disciple I must be free to follow, and that means freeing myself from the bondage that ego has agreed to live in. We must now explore this call to freedom at the heart of conversion.

CONVERSION AS A CALL TO FREEDOM

"When I first heard about the Enneagram," we might hear someone say, " I looked into it, but it seemed so negative. It always seemed to be pointing to the things that I do wrong. Well, that's all I heard when I was growing up. I figured I had had enough of that. There must be more to spirituality than that." I have a great deal of sympathy and understanding for this kind of a statement (heaven knows, I've said it enough myself!), and if that is the extent to which the Enneagram is taught, then this person has every right to walk away from it. I recognize that the system is designed to take head-on the things we "do wrong." I also recognize that this is only half of the issue. To look at the Enneagram as a tool that merely shows us what is most wrong with us is a misperception, to say the least. In itself, negativity offers us no advantage to conversion whatsoever, and in fact it is as much part of the problem of our sinfulness as anything. As a result it will always be necessary to use the Enneagram with self-compassion. To do anything else is to jeopardize the conversion we seek.

But the Enneagram, while pointing to the negative, is not negative itself. As a spiritual tool for transformation, the Enneagram can be a very positive and powerful servant of the Gospel. First, it calls each of us to break the self-centered illusions we structure for ourselves. That in itself is good news. However, it then offers us a course of action and a direction in which to move that enables conversion to take root and bear fruit. This course of action has to

present

do with how the Enneagram presents us with a call to freedom.

At the heart of this call to freedom is the exhortation to live in the *present.* It is only in the present moment that I can experience the fullness that life has to offer. Ego spends much of its time in the past, regretting what it didn't do, feeling guilty about what it should have done, complaining about what was done to it. Ego spends much of its time in the future, plotting its coming successes, planning its vindications and revenges, worrying about its lack of adequate preparation. Ego spends the remainder of its time asleep, in mindless addictive behavior. To be present, really present, I must awaken the true self. I must choose to be conscious, to act for what is happening now, to feel the complete range of emotions present, to think of what the moment actually places before me. If I want to be free, I have to realize that I can only be free in the present. Neither you nor I has ever experienced freedom any other way.

Our society has conditioned most of us to be dissatisfied with doing the present thing. Most of us have bought into the illusion that the good, successful person should be able to do two, three, or four things at once. If I am trying to do more than one thing at this moment, I am probably doing nothing. When we meet a person who is truly conscious of what she or he is doing, we can tell the difference in a moment. In those moments when we have cleared our minds and have been fully present to what was before us, we also have experienced the difference of consciousness. Unfortunately, it is for so many of us an all too rare occasion.

To consciously choose to live and act in the present moment opens me to the potential of grace. The Kingdom is never far; it is in our midst. But ego does not see the Kingdom. This moment is the moment of *kairos*, the appropriate moment for the inbreaking of the Reign. To be able to respond to it I will have to have the freedom of consciousness. When I meet the call of Jesus in my daily life, it is seldom written in bold letters on billboards; it is seldom even put in a religious language. Most often it is in the person I mindlessly passed by, in the unkind word I thoughtlessly spoke, in the indifference I had to the emotional state of myself or another. If I missed those moments of grace, what benefit is my religious language and my planned spiritual practices?

If the Gospel calls me to be the wise steward, the disciple who can respond at any moment to the master's return, then consciousness is the key. If conversion is the breaking out of the structures of bondage imposed upon me by ego, then I am called to make choices that "produce fruits worthy of repentance."

The Gospel call of conversion is a call to seek liberation. In logical sequence this is first a call to the liberation of ourselves as individuals. In using the Enneagram to help bring this about, there is the need that each of us has to begin seeing connections. It is all too easy for me to live my life as if it were a series of random snapshots, one scene disconnected from all the others. I am not aware that everything within me is connected. My thoughts are connected to my feelings, even when I am not aware of my feelings. The reactions that I have in my body are connected to the rest of me. This moment is connected to the one that preceeded it. This response I make is connected to past responses in similar circumstances. And so on. The Gurdjieff Work speaks of something called *sclf-observation.* We need to be sensitive to the experiences of our lives. It is crucial that we are able to observe patterns in our lives. When I find myself doing something that I have done before, and I am aware that I did not choose to do it, I have discovered a life pattern. Such patterns are *always* significant. If I didn't choose it, where did it come from? If I do not know where it came from, if I do not know its motivational source, then I have a broken connection. I must consciously make that connection. The broken connections in our experiences are perhaps only little invitations offered to us that we might see, but they are not insignificant. The ability to notice the negative and positive emotions present in my life, to see the random patterns of my thoughts, to be aware of the reactions my body, my mind, my whole being, make as I go through this day, these are significant moments of grace.

In recognizing patterns and consciously pulling myself back to the present, I am able to evaluate these patterns from a new vantage point. If the pattern is harmless, in the sense that there is no manipulation or violence present to myself or others, I am still able to decide if it is the kind of behavior I want. If I find that in fact the conditioned pattern I have discovered is in some way destructive, I have the opportunity to choose to let go of it in order to embrace a more graced reality.

Living consciously in the moment will enable me to choose new behavior that will free my spirit. The most important choices I make in life are all made from the conscious moment. No one has ever made a true decision of faith from conditioned behavior. To be willing to turn my life over to God is to know my life for what it is, and that is only possible consciously in the present. To be willing to give myself to another in love is only possible when that act of giving is free. Otherwise I will call some form of manipulation "love" and continue to use other people in some way. To truly act justly is only possible when I have freely relinquished my hold on the various forms of power that keep others in oppression, something I do not just "fall into." These kinds of *free actions* are the very heart of Gospel holiness, and they are the fruits of conscious living.

If the call to liberation logically begins with the individual, it does not necessarily begin there *practically.* In reality, at the very moment that I am called to free myself I am also called to liberate all of creation. The two cannot be separated. I cannot wait until I get "my own act together." My liberation must extend itself to the entire world. What is more, in true consciousness this will manifest itself as a natural flow. If I am seeing the connections that give me the potential for graced living, I cannot but see the disconnections that still hold the world in bondage.

In attempting to live consciously I soon discover that the world is caught in as much addictive behavior as I am. Society often works out of the same destructive behavior patterns that I have come to see in my own life. If I am greedy and seek only the interests of ego, society also seeks only to protect itself and grow at the expense of those less fortunate. If I am prejudiced toward what my own upbringing has conditioned me to, society also hates and fears anything that seems to be other than its consensus trance. If I can project my own uncertainties and inadequacies onto my enemy next door or across town, society can bring untold damage upon itself and the world by waging war with what is currently passing as the epitome of evil. If my unrecognized need for personal power can endanger me and all those I interact with, society's need for power is just as capable of oppressing and using and destroying all that stands in its way.

To begin making social connections is just as important as making personal connections, and in fact the two are often part of the same process. With each I shatter the bonds of addictive sleep that keep me from living consciously and gracefully. I also discover that I am, to use a familiar phrase, no longer part of the problem, but I have become part of the solution. Often the very same actions of conversion that bring me deeper into discipleship are actions that further the inbreaking of the Reign of God.

This process of liberation whereby I become the wise steward that Jesus speaks of is a process that demands my initiative. I cannot bury the one talent I have been given just because it seems like the safer thing to do. Consciousness is ultimately an *action*, not a reaction. It is an action that no one else will do for me. I am the only one responsible for my freedom. My parents are not, nor is my pastor, nor the sisters who taught me in elementary school, nor the government, nor the Church. The only way to escape this kind of responsibility is not to choose it, but then the bridegroom comes and I was off buying oil for my lamp. I find I missed the celebration, and while another moment might come, my loss of this opportunity of grace is decisive.

For this reason the way I proceed in the process of liberation must be ruthless. This does not mean I must be violent with myself, but it means that I can never afford to underestimate the addictive nature of the ego. I cannot take anything for granted when it comes to the distorted aspects of my motivational core. I must root them out, and not just once, but again and again. Automatic conditioning will return if given the chance. That is why I cannot rest on past accomplishments. Because I did something once in response to grace is something to celebrate, but it is not something to take for granted.

This in itself is enough to explain why conversion must be a process, and not simply an experience. Perhaps at one point in my life I decided to return to church, or I was able to stop drinking, or I agreed to go to marriage counseling, or whatever I determine was an act of conversion. However, it does not mean that I am now finished. The founder of my own spiritual tradition, Francis of Assisi, said: "Let us begin to serve the Lord God, for up to now we have made little or no progress."[16] Does that mean that Francis

---

[16]   *The First Life of St. Francis* by Thomas of Celano, # 103.   See: Habig, Marion A. Ed., *St. Francis of Assisi: Writings and Early Biographies.* Chicago: Franciscan Herald Press, 1973. p. 318.

really thought that he had previously done nothing? No, it means that Francis realized that in this present moment there is *something* to do, and I cannot look back. If I am called to live the spiritual life ruthlessly, it must *always* be with compassion. In seeking transformation and conversion there is no room for that kind of perfectionism that is really a self-violence. It is, however, most unfortunate that we were likely trained to pursue the spiritual life in just that way. If we are going through our lives continuously comparing ourselves and our actions against the ideal image of ourselves that we have formed in our minds, and then judging ourselves as bad because we have not measured up, not only are we actually frustrating the real conversion process, we are most likely driving ourselves deeper into self-hatred and the slavery to ego that we are called to abandon.

There is also the need here for a serious warning. If I take on the Enneagram out of a perfectionism model of spirituality, I will be taking on a harsh taskmaster. The reason is simple. The addictive patterns of ego are there in our lives, and they are myriad. If I cannot be compassionate with myself (not to mention others), I will simply use the Enneagram as one more way of holding myself in bondage. This unfortunately can also be true of the Gospel. If I hear the Gospel mandate to walk the extra mile, turn the other cheek, and forgive my brother or sister seventy times seven, and judge myself as bad because I have not done it "perfectly," whatever else I might have done, I have turned it into something that no longer resembles the person of Jesus it is supposed to reveal.

The ministry of Jesus, as we have seen, was one of compassion. The very call of Jesus to forgive one another so often is born out of the need for reconciliation, not judgment. The Enneagram too is to be a tool of compassion. It is first to show us the need to be self-compassionate, to show us that much of what traps us is not of our conscious choosing, and not something we need to *blame* ourselves for. While the recognition of consciousness calls us to change what we do, it does not call us to judge ourselves as evil.

Secondly, it is to be a tool that aids us in our call to be compassionate to others. If my conscious awareness can help me to disengage from my own self-judgment, it can also help me disengage from the actions of others. What for so long has seemed to be what others were "doing to me" now simply becomes what they do. It is most likely not directed at me personally, and even if it is, it is no longer something the ego feels it must defend. If I can see how difficult it is to extricate myself from my fundamental addictive core, I can also recognize the need to give others the necessary space for conversion.

If living in the present, being open to the *kairos* moment of grace, consciously choosing to break the patterns of the addictive ego, is so graceful and so fruitful, why have I apparently had such little success in seeing it in my life? Is the process of holiness and discipleship really so difficult? What if I do not feel capable of a superhuman effort? Actually the key to our freedom is not something great or complicated;

nor is it far from any of us. The necessary key to the liberation of grace is *surrender.*

SURRENDER AS THE FUNDAMENTAL SPIRITUAL EXPERIENCE

If there is anything we must come to learn in our pursuit of the spiritual life, it is the importance of *surrender.* Without this experience, all of what has been said up to now would be of little use to any of us.

I have tried to present the importance of recognizing the patterns of conditioned responses that underlie our actions, and the need to identify these as connected to a core motivational distortion that keeps the false self attached to fundamental addictive behavior. I have pointed out the need to break this pattern of slavery to ego by the conscious choosing of the graced response in this present moment. I have stressed the need to take the initiative in this, pursuing the Reign of God in every opportunity. However, if we were to stop there we would not have yet embraced the complete process that the Enneagram envisions. If we were to stop there it would not be long before ego would once more make claims upon our lives.

That it is not possible to stop here, not possible to simply let our conscious and truer self take over for ego, is perhaps the clearest acknowledgement that the Enneagram is not in the final analysis a psychology, but is in fact a *spirituality,* in the truest sense of the word. To move beyond consciousness and into surrender requires a jump that cannot be taken except through some decision of faith. No matter what my religious language, no matter what my spiritual experience, surrender recognizes that there is something beyond me that I cannot control, and in fact which I desperately need.

At some point each of us must come to the realization that it is not totally possible to free myself merely through my own choosing. To begin with, I cannot bring myself to total consciousness. I discover that my core motivations are too deeply rooted to the false self. My conditioning has been years in the making, the habits and patterns of ego intricately fashioned again and again in the most nuanced of circumstances. I discover that I have literally hundreds of options when it comes to using my core life distortion. To simply stop one type of behavior might well open me up to another just as addictive, and if I break this there may well be another. Each one is a little more subtle, a little more justifiable.

Even the best of efforts are open to distortion as well. We must remember what Paul recognized centuries ago. "What I do, I do not understand. For I do not do what I want, but I do what I hate." (Rom 7:15) With the best of intentions I begin to pursue freedom, having a well-reflected perception of what that means, only to discover that when I get there, it is not what I thought at all. The end I envisioned was after all a misperception. While the action might have been praiseworthy, I finish it only to discover I am still under the power of the false self.

Perhaps I am image- and success-oriented, and I have come to recognize my motivations centered around what the Enneagram refers to as the THREE space. I have come to realize that I am too clothes conscious, that I wear only the best that I can afford and always look sharp. I decide to break out of this trap. I give away some of my best sweaters and content myself with older ones, hoping this will free me from my attachment. To my surprise, however, no one notices the difference. I have kept my sweaters in such good shape that they really appear new. Well, that says something about me, of course. Not everyone would have such care for their appearance. But after a while I begin to drop subtle remarks about the sweaters I have given away, not actually coming out and telling people what I did (of course, I'm not that kind of person!), but still deep within hoping they notice.

So what have I done? I still believe that I am pursuing a worthy goal, breaking out of the trap of my image-consciousness, but perhaps not realizing that in more subtle ways I am still locked into images of myself, images of the kind of person I believe myself to be. As ruthless as I am with Holy Suspicion, it is vain for me to think that I will catch every slip of self-deception. Left to myself, the chances are far greater that I will end up repeating new forms of the same old patterns, or in fact, I might actually be pursuing the wrong goal entirely. So often what begins well ends in new forms of entrapment.

We stand in need, therefore, of something beyond us. It is not just something useful; it is necessary. It is not just something that will speed up the process of transformation and conversion. It is instead something at the very heart of transformation, something within the very essence of conversion. It is what J. G. Bennett refers to as *help.*[17] It is what I have called throughout this book, and what the Christian tradition has always called *grace.* Grace is the very life of God around us, the gift of God initiated within us. It is the working of the Spirit within each moment, the manifestation of a love so profound there is no distancing ourselves from it. This grace is freely offered to us in faith, won for us, in our Christian belief, once and for all by Jesus. We can reject it (and sadly often do), but we cannot stifle its drive to win our hearts.

Theologians down through the centuries have sought to categorize grace, dividing it up in different ways, stipulating what kind of grace is at work here, what kind there. I do not say they are wrong, but I do not choose to differentiate it. It is less important that we intellectualize about it than that we are able to recognize it and accept it in our daily lives, in the *kairos* moment. Grace is at work now as you are reading this. Something is presently happening to you at this moment that is presenting you with the opportunity to choose to live within the Reign. If it is not what you are reading, then place the book aside and respond to the invitation, for there is nothing more important now than focusing on what is being offered.

Grace, as I have said, is tied to faith. Without faith the reception of grace is not possible. That is why I have said that each of us needs to be pursuing a tradition (even if it is one of our own making!), for

---

[17] Bennett, J. G. *Transformation.* Charles Town, WV: Claymont Communications, 1978. pp. 47-57.

it is only when I have something ultimate to believe in that I can surrender to grace. I do not mean to imply that traditions are interchangeable, one being as good as another. If I felt that, I would believe in nothing. The one who has truly found a place to stand in faith is rightfully convinced of her or his beliefs. Still, each one respects the reality that many sincere and maturing people have come to stand in other traditions. Without the ability to have this respect for others, a manifestation of compassion, the depth of one's own faith stance could rightly be questioned.

By faith I do not mean to imply simply a set of intellectual belief statements. There is, of course, a place for credal statements, and a place for a well thought-out theological investigation of Mystery. But I cannot confuse that kind of analytical activity with the lived experience of faith. The faith I speak of is the faith called forth by Jesus in the gospels. It is a faith that is born in decision and commitment, a faith that is a manifestation of profound trust in life and what lies beyond life. It is a faith that is seeking the Kingdom, seeking discipleship, seeking to live and act in God's will.

The attitude of trust that I refer to is crucial. Trust is the *fundamental spiritual attitude.* We have already seen that the gospels understood faith and trust as the same reality. This trust that I am called to possess in God, in life, in others, in myself, is so important that without it, true conversion, true holiness is not possible. Without it there can be no transformation, for I will be unable to open myself enough to let the necessary grace in. The paradoxical thing is, however, that this trust itself is brought about in response to grace, in response to God's invitation to life.

Nor is the paradox ended there. It is also true that part of my stance in trust calls me to recognize that the possession of trust is not enough in itself. Trust is the attitude of faith, but the attitude is not sufficient. As much as I can, through conscious action, break out of old patterns and learn to trust myself, at some level I still must recognize myself, standing on my own, as untrustworthy. This takes us back to what Paul referred to as *sarx*, which literally means flesh. Paul does not mean to refer to the body in a physical sense, but to the whole person trying to live solely on ones own. "For I know that good does not dwell in me, that is, in my flesh. The willing is ready at hand, but doing the good is not." (Rom 7:18) In other words, when all is said and done, I am still a creature; I am mortal (made for death), limited in time and space and energy, limited in power, even over myself. Even my faith is limited. Like the father of the boy with a mute spirit, each of us must cry out, "I do believe, help my unbelief." (Mk 9:24)

Trust, then, the fundamental spiritual attitude, implies the need for surrender, the *fundamental spiritual experience.* Surrender is the heart of the spiritual life. Without it I only stand in isolation, in defiance, in uncertainty. Without it what I call trust is only a misshapen reality. You will perhaps remember Murphy's Law: Whatever can go wrong will go wrong, and in the direction that does the most damage. Murphy's Law and the hundreds of corollaries we find scattered around are meant to be humorous, and they are. But if we were to take Murphy's Law as our philosophy of life, we would be embracing a radical mistrust. If I view life as so arbitrary and devious as to frustrate my every attempt to meet it, I will not be able to respond to grace, nor will I make room for the celebration of life's goodness. If I cannot surrender to life's basic goodness, my only options are to fall back in a fundamental survival stance, or to forge ahead in order to grasp and cling to what I can get. In short, without surrender I can stand only in ego, the *false self.*

Ego denies the need for surrender; instead it holds out for something else. Surely, ego says, I do not have to give this up. Surely this will not die. At least I can preserve this possession. I will not be able to survive without it -- the self-deception of an addiction.

Every spiritual action is an action of surrender. No matter how small, no matter how great, every attempt to turn to God involves surrender. If I wish to discern an action or a decision, I could well ask where it involves surrender. If I am not letting something of ego fall away, I might well question my direction.

I cannot truly *love*, for instance, if I cannot surrender. How could I love you if I cannot let myself be known by you? How could I really give myself in love if I am incapable of surrendering the personal boundaries of my protection in order to become vulnerable? How can it be love if there is only taking and not giving? And why should I expect it to be any different when I speak of wanting to love God?

I cannot seek *justice* unless I surrender. Until I recognize that I am to some extent unjust myself, and must therefore relinquish my own self-seeking power, I cannot speak with any authenticity about justice. How can I seek to bring justice to others, to the world, to the Church, or to my spouse, if I cannot let go of my own self-righteousness? I cannot seek *truth* unless I am honestly willing to be changed by truth.

I cannot *pray* if in my prayer I cling to my pride.

I cannot seek *faith and discipleship* unless I am willing to admit that it will inevitably ask me to renounce all for the sake of the Kingdom.

That word *renounce*, of course, has become a painful word to many. While it is true that in an earlier spiritual discipline renunciation was distorted, often causing violence and manipulation in the name of spirituality, it is also true that renunciation is part and parcel of the Gospel message. Holy Suspicion would ask us to recognize that often renunciation is not popular simply because we don't want to give anything up. It is sad (and an indictment upon our society) that renunciation has little to do with our present consensus trance.

Therefore, when we speak of surrender we need to know that we are speaking of *death*. Ultimately there can be no surrender that does not involve death, the loss and ending of something. Death, of course, always begins with life. There is something here and now that is alive to me. I want it; I think I need it, and maybe I do. I have at least become used to its living with me, and often to the extent that a part of me or all of me would seem threatened without it. I have, as the Gurdjieff Work would say, become *identified* with it. I think somehow it *is* me. Surren-

der is the willingness to let go of what I recognize life
to be.

Death is everything it's cracked up to be! When
I speak of death I include mortal death, my own and
that of the people I love. This is the greatest death,
the death we most fear, to the extent that most would
rather not even look at it, or be reminded about it.
This death involves our greatest grieving. Death,
however, is also experienced each day in hundreds of
smaller and less tangible ways. Sometimes we recognize them as deaths only by our grieving at their
passing. We grieve the loss of our power; we grieve
the loss of our vitality. We grieve our sicknesses, our
aging, our discouragements. We mourn our failures;
we regret our rejections. We suffer the pain of our
loneliness, and so on. Death itself is not sin, but as
Scripture attests, the two are not far from each other.
My fear of death brings with it alienation, resentment,
revenge, etc. I so fear the loss of my life, of what I
perceive life to be, that I would go to any lengths to
preserve it -- or so I am counseled by the false self.

Death cannot be escaped. Life cannot be
preserved. This is true on the wide screen of my
existence. It is also true of the simplest of realities.
Even my time is dying. I cannot hold on to it. As
much as I want the greatest, most joyful, most profound, most ecstatic experiences of my life to stay
forever, they stubbornly drift into memory. At least in
my finite perception, they are gone.

But for all this, death is not an enemy. Death is
not the end of life; it is a part of life. Death is
something worked into the very fabric of life. It is
worked into the very fabric of conversion and trans-

formation.   I have said that conversion involves conscious choosing, but every true choice is a death. When I choose, I must leave something behind.   If there is nothing I am seeing fall away, then what choice have I made?   Perhaps I am still holding out for the possibility that I will get it all, if not now, maybe later.   Perhaps I am still claiming to be without limits.   Perhaps I do not need faith.   Perhaps I need only myself -- or so I am fooled by the false self.

It is true that death surrounds me, but it does not have to overwhelm me.   Faith itself has an answer for death: death is the stuff out of which *resurrection* is made.   Resurrection.   We think of it as something that happened to Jesus, as something that will happen to us after we die, or at the end of time, or beyond this life.   Yes, this is all true.   And if we suffer the hundreds of deaths this day, are we not to look for resurrection here too?   If death is a part of life, cannot resurrection be a part of life as well?

One thing is very clear.   Resurrection cannot exist without death, contrary to popular opinion. Without something to die, there is nothing to rise. We hold out for a deathless resurrection, but this is impossible.   We would like to get the incalculable wealth of the diamond without having to pay the price.   We would like to get the treasure in the field -- *and* the field -- without having to sell all we have in order to buy it.   It is an illusion.

Resurrection is *only* death transformed.   It is not the next step in the extended sequence.   It is simply seeing death as it truly is.   It is life where life seemed impossible.   It is recognizing that it was possible all along.   Resurrection is not one thing changing into another; it is the transformation of what always was into what it was meant to be, its essence moving to a whole new plane of existence.

It must be said, however, that resurrection is not an inevitable reality. If that were the case, creation would not truly have freedom. Death does not *necessarily* have to come to transformation any more than I am compelled to come to conversion. On any given day there is plenty of death around us. Our newspapers are full of it. It permeates our experiences. I am not saying that all this death is automatically transformed. (I do not know if transformation is ever automatic.) What I am suggesting is that all death is *potentially* transformable. The death that comes to be resurrection is the death that is *surrendered*. That is why surrender is the key to conversion. That is why surrender is fundamental to the spiritual life.

In Christian theology what I have been talking about here is called the *paschal mystery*. Life, death, resurrection -- these are the elements of the salvation we have in Christ. Jesus did not die, did not *live*, to keep us from death. Jesus died so that resurrection might be released. Jesus surrendered in time so that our surrendering might forever be fruitful for the Kingdom. It is indeed a *mystery*, but it is not beyond the realm of our experience. It is, however, only experienced in faith.

That we share in the mystery of Christ's resurrection is witnessed to in the experience of the early Church.

Or are you unaware that we who were baptized into Christ Jesus were baptized into his death? We were indeed buried with him through baptism into death, so that, just as Christ was raised from the dead by the glory of the Father, we too might live in newness of life. For if we have grown into union with him through a death like his, we shall also be united with him in the resurrection. We know that our old self was crucified with him, so that our sinful body might be done away with, that we might no longer be in slavery to sin. For a dead person has been absolved from sin. If, then, we have died with Christ, we believe that we shall also live with him. We know that Christ, raised from the dead, dies no more; death no longer has power over him. As to his death, he died to sin once and for all; as to his life, he lives for God. Consequently, you too must think of yourselves as being dead to sin and living for God in Christ Jesus. (Rom. 6:3-11)

Paul came to this experience not through any knowledge of the Enneagram, but through his knowledge of the Risen Christ. We too are called each day to witness in our lives to the paschal mystery of Jesus. We are brought to the realization of this mystery only through faith, and not through any tool, neither the Enneagram nor any other. But in the hands of a faithful and wise steward, the Enneagram can be a powerful invitation of grace in the ruthless pursuit of transformation.

FOUR

THE WISE AND FAITHFUL STEWARD

THE STORY: THE JAR OF FULFILLMENT

Two travelers of renowned holiness were making their way on journey when they found themselves in an expansive desert area. They wandered for some time, growing in exhaustion, hunger, and thirst. Finally they stumbled upon an isolated area of lush vegetation, and discovered at its center a lively, bubbling spring. They had only begun to rest from the weary journey when an old man appeared. At first the two met the man with extreme caution and suspicion, for they could not understand how someone would come to be in that out-of-the-way place. Yet, as they had decided to spend the night there, they found they had a lengthy time to speak to him, and actually came to enjoy his company. He spoke with a candid friendliness, and seemed to possess a rich enthusiasm for life.

As the two travelers gradually opened up, they began to share with the old man many of their hopes and dreams. They explained to him the nature of their quest, and how they had come to be on this journey. The old man listened attentively, and encouraged them in their endeavor.

While one of the travelers had gone off to the spring, the old man approached the other. Speaking in a low and serious manner, he asked, "Tell me, what would you say is the purpose of life?"

She answered, "That is easy. Life's purpose is the pursuit of truth."

"A marvelous answer," the old man replied, "and for that answer I would like to present you with a gift." He took from what seemed to be nowhere an earthen jar. Handing it to her, he said, "This jar is a very precious gift. It is a jar of fulfillment. At each pouring it can give forth a measure of the precious commodity which you seek."

The traveler eagerly took the jar, and was able to hide it in her belongings before her companion returned.

Not much later that evening, it happened that the old man was alone with the other traveler. In the course of their conversation he posed the same question to him. "What is the purpose of life?"

The man was as quick to respond as his companion had been. "The purpose of life is to give and receive love."

"A marvelous answer," replied the old man, "and with that answer comes a gift. This is a jar of fulfillment," he said, presenting a duplicate jar to the traveler, "and from it you can always pour forth a measure of that which you seek."

The second traveler reverently took the gift, and carefully placed it with his other possessions. Both travelers spent peaceful nights, and early the next morning they bid farewell to their newfound friend without, they were later to realize, ever learning his name. Their journey now seemed more resolute, as they agreed to proceed homeward with as much haste as possible.

Having finally come to the end of the long and weary trip, both pilgrims were tired and sore. Once home, the one traveler felt it best to rest a little, but first found time to prepare a special place in the living room for the precious jar. It remained there for many years to come, a great attraction to friends, and truly the prized possession of the house.

The other pilgrim, once in the town, although tired, found little time for resting. The traveler hastened to the village square and, finding a place among the poor and disheartened, began to pour out measure by measure from the jar's unlimited contents.

THE SPIRITUAL PARADOX

Having been raised in the generation of the 1960s I can still hear echoing in my mind the words of Joni Mitchell:

I've looked at life from both sides now,
    from give and take, and still somehow
It's life's illusions I recall.
    I really don't know life at all.

It seems that life presents us with two different sides so often. They appear as contradictions, two separate poles of experience. Sometimes life seems like it is indeed giving, but sometimes it appears to take. Sometimes it appears as light; sometimes it is enveloped in darkness. Sometimes I am inside my experiences; sometimes I view them objectively from without.

Another song of the '60s, written by Pete Seeger and quoting the Book of Ecclesiastes (3:1-8), intones, "To everything, turn, turn, turn; there is a season, turn turn, turn." Our experiences often lead us in a kind of merry-go-round of opposing forces: life and death, planting and uprooting, killing and healing, and so on. And when we stand before God we bring our doubts and uncertainties about this polarity of experience. We are like Tevye in "Fiddler on the Roof," weighing the contradictions that stand before us. "On the one hand..., on the other hand...," Our discernment seems to continuously weigh the pros and cons in the balance, hoping that sooner or later some light will go on that will show us the clear way. Too often this waiting seems like a futile exercise, and we begin to despair of any answer whatsoever. Moreover, our prayer is frustrated by the realization that our experiences of God seem to be as contradictory as anything else.

To enter into surrender, the fundamental spiritual experience, means that I acknowledge that there is something beyond contradiction. To enter into surrender changes the very nature of contradiction. In surrender the opposing poles of experience are no longer contradictions; they are instead *paradox.* Paradox is a profound spiritual reality. Paradox opens me to mystery. It asks me to take a stance as creature, bound by limits and mortality, and as creature to stand before my creator, before the transcendent reality I meet and in some way participate in. It is a meeting and participation that lies always beyond complete understanding, and certainly beyond adequate expression.

Throughout the course of the human spiritual adventure, the articulation of paradox has been the function of *myth.* When we hear this word we often think of something like "fable" or "tale," because myths most often are presented in primal story form. We have come, however, often to hear the word as implying something that is not true. If anything, the opposite is the case. Myth is the attempt to express what we feel to be the truest part of us in an imaged language that expands our understanding beyond what mere concept will allow.

Mythic structure in its most profound expression seeks to reconcile the opposition of contradictory experience. It attempts through the use of the depths of creative imagination to show not only how two opposing factors can be found legitimately in the same reality, but also how their presence there actually opens that reality to the potential for transcendence. This reconciliation through mythic structure could be seen as directly connected with Gurdjieff's understanding of the Law of Trinity. Within the encounter of every event of our lives, there stands opposite the event a contrary force that I meet as contradiction. Ouspensky quotes Gurdjieff as saying:

> Man, in the normal state natural to him, is taken as a *duality*. He consists entirely of dualities or "pairs of opposites." All man's sensations, impressions, feelings, thoughts, are divided into positive and negative, useful and harmful, necessary and unnecessary, good and bad, pleasant and unpleasant. The work of centers proceeds under the sign of this division. Thoughts oppose feelings. Moving impulses oppose instinctive craving for quiet. This is the duality in

which proceed all the perceptions, all the reactions, the whole life of man.[1]

Yet, in the surrendering to a third force, that contradiction is not only reconciled, it is also transcended. When this third force is made present, I am in the midst of a holy moment. Gurdjieff referred to these three forces as Holy Affirming, Holy Denying, and Holy Neutralizing.[2] It is, as I implied earlier, a *creative* moment in the fullest sense of the word.

A fundamental example of this gives a better understanding of the spiritual adventure. Throughout this book I have been hinting at a paradoxical relationship that exists between will and grace, between what I can do in regard to my response to life and what ultimately lies beyond my doing. On the one hand, I can act. I am able to decide and respond to the events of life. I am responsible for the choices that I make. Not only can I act, but in the realm in which it is made available, I *must* act. If I do not act when possible, I run the risk of frustrating the Reign of God. All of this points to the primacy of the will in terms of my own spiritual project of discipleship.

On the other hand, it is just as true to say that I cannot act. There is a way in which I must admit that I am truly powerless to control the forces of life. I made no choice about my primary life distortion, nor can I cash it in for another. I cannot control events

---

[1] Ouspensky, *op. cit.,* p. 281.

[2] See, for instance: Speeth, *op. cit.,* pp. 44-45.

around me. Often even the simplest things are beyond my ability to manage. Moreover, nothing I can do ultimately will enable me to overcome death in its hundreds of variations. To claim surrender as being fundamental to the spiritual life is to point to the primacy of grace. Without grace there can be no discipleship.

I can act; I cannot act. Both are true statements. I am totally dependent upon my will; I am totally dependent upon God's grace. We live within this paradox, at one time clearly recognizing the truth of the first statement, at another convinced of the validity of the second. But we cannot remain for long straddling both sides of the fence. We need only look at the fragmentation caused within the faith community in the 16th century over justification by works and justification by faith to recognize that extended duality is not fruitful for the Reign. Contradiction must be transformed into paradox. The affirming and denying forces must be surrendered into transcendence.

Jesus was the master of paradox. For people of faith this should come as no surprise, since paradox is of God. The problem isn't with Jesus; it is with us. Ego resists paradox, for paradox always implies surrender, which always means the ego's death. The false self wants it "both ways," or "my way," or "no way," all of which are excluded by paradox. If we listen to the Gospel and we hear contradictions, we may well ask who is listening, my self or my ego? If we listen to the Gospel and recognize paradox, we may rejoice in God's goodness.

The epitome of the paradoxical nature of Jesus is found in his use of the parable. A parable is not simply a nice little story that Jesus tells us to teach us something about God. In fact, for ego, there is very little that is "nice" in a parable to begin with, for the parable is asking us for some type of surrender. I present here two parables that, at one level, point to the contradiction between will and grace. Of course, at the level of surrender they both are saying the same thing.

The first parable is the Parable of the Talents (Mt 25:14-30). It is perhaps unfortunate that the word "talent" is used, since we often immediately think of a natural ability or gift. This line of thinking throws us off what the parable is speaking to, for a talent is a sum of money, in fact, a very large sum of money. In the story three people are given varying sums of money for the sake of investment. The first two invest wisely, and for their efforts they each double the sum. The third servant, "out of fear," buries the money. He thinks the master will be content to receive it back safely. This was, however, no time for caution. He is not rewarded; instead he is reprimanded. More than that, he is thrown into the darkness outside. What did the man do to earn such treatment? Certainly he did nothing *wrong*, his own caution protected him from that. But he did not *act* with initiative. He was not a *wise* steward. The Reign of God was calling him to make a choice, in fact, several choices. It was time for an action of will. And the parable is very clear that there is a terrible price to pay for not heeding the nature of the moment.

The second parable we can look at is the Parable of the Workers in the Vineyard (Mt 20:1-16). This is a vexing parable for many of us, because it seems so unfair. Especially those of us who have stood up for the rights of workers and have been advocates of fair wages hear this parable with consternation, or outright anger. The story, as we know, tells of an owner of a vineyard who goes out early in the morning to hire workers. Throughout the day he makes several trips to the place where hiring takes place, sending more and more workers into the vineyard. Finally, he even sends workers into the fields who will only be able to work for an hour. In the end, however, everyone gets the same wage, the one who worked for an hour as well as the one who worked all day long in the heat of the day.

Of course, we realize, the owner was not unjust. He paid the agreed upon wage to all. He did not cheat anyone. The problem, as the first workers point out, is that he was *unfair*. The fair and proportionate thing to do would be to pay according to a scale of the work done. The owner is not fair; he is *generous*. He pays out lavishly, beyond proportion. He can be generous because he is free. No one had a *right* to work in the vineyard. Their entrance was solely by gratuitous invitation. What we also realize is that the amount of work done is of little account. The amount of action, the amount of energy, is of little use in terms of the payment. That comes, not from the effort, but from the very commitment to enter into the vineyard.

It is even more revealing when we consider that the most likely original context of the parable was a situation where Jesus was contrasting God's invitation to the "keepers of the Law," like the Pharisees, who had been working on perfection a long time, with the invitation offered to the sinners and those beyond the Law's protection. The latter were new on the scene, the invitation having come only with the preaching of Jesus. Not only had they simply not been working, but they were sinners. Their actions were actually counter to the Law. How could they get the same "reward" as those who had been making such an extended effort for so long? The answer is simple; it is not a matter of effort, but of grace. There is *no one* who deserves the Reign. It is a free gift. Effort cannot earn it. No amount of action, no matter how timely, can produce it.

Here is a fundamental paradox of salvation, and of course, of conversion. What sort of statement can be made to help us understand this mystery? Where is the point of surrender in the apparent contradiction between grace and will? I believe that it is in the experiential knowledge of this statement: *The best things in life are free -- at a terrible price.*

Grace abounds! That is an essential realization in the Christian life. I never have to go far to find God's offer of life. It is as close to me as the air I breathe. But I do not dare pass through it mindlessly. Grace demands a response of will. I must choose to accept grace and cooperate with it. I cannot presume my participation in it, but I must be like the wise steward, always prepared to seize the opportunity, always ready for the inbreaking of the Reign.

The Gurdjieff tradition uses a different language. It speaks of something called the Work. In the words of J.G. Bennett:

One great advantage of the word "Work" is this: we don't really separate the Work from the worker. If we see that it is so, we have something very important: when we use the word "Work" we are not talking about ourselves, we're not talking about what we do and yet we ourselves and what we do are there; and the Work is also what is done to us, its action upon us. It is altogether true to say that the Work is an action upon us. It is also true to say that the Work is what we do. It is also true to say the Work is the reality of our whole life.[3]

What is implied in all this is the importance of an ongoing discernment in the process of our lives. Responding to the invitation of the Reign sometimes requires me to make an effort. Yet sometimes there will be no effort or action that will help. Sometimes the Reign of God requires receptivity. I must surrender to forces I have no control over, not in resignation, but in faith, hope, and love.

Every moment calls for discernment. We sometimes think of discernment as coming into play only when we are faced with major life decisions. We consider a career change, contemplate a marriage, question a religious vocation -- it is time for discernment. Yet we cannot afford to bring out discernment

------

[3] Bennett, J.G. *The Sevenfold Work*. Charles Town, WV: Claymont Communications, 1979. p. 17.

only in the big moments, as if it were the secret weapon we only use in dire circumstances. We must be in *constant* discernment. If I cannot discern this moment, as simple and inconsequential as it might seem, what makes me think I will be able to trust my discernment in something big? The reality is that this moment is not inconsequential. This moment is of ultimate significance.

Discernment requires a response of my whole person to the circumstances of my life. Many people approach discernment as if it were a mental activity. They list all the pros and cons, weigh their options, filter them through their understanding of Scripture, bounce their range of ideas off directors and friends, and hope to come up with a certain answer. The process essentially happens from the neck up. When the results of their efforts fail to satisfy their longing for certitude, they become anxious and mistrusting. They often have not listened closely to their emotions. They have not searched their physical reactions. They have not been sensitive to conditioned patterns. They have not listened closely to their dreams, or to other imaginative resources. Nor have they searched the event involved for their own motivational roots. The use of our intellectual center is essential in a holistic approach to life, but a strictly cognitive discernment can be easily controlled by the false self, causing us either to arrive at a pre-determined end, or to arrive at no real end at all.

The other problem with such a discernment is that usually by the time the process is complete the moment is gone. A systematic cognitive discernment is an analytical process that takes time. Perhaps in a major life decision I will have the time to run through the complete process, but in the discernment that *kairos* asks, I seldom have that luxury. I must become sensitive to reading my whole person immediately, intellect, emotions, and moving/instinctual center, and then acting with initiative. A true holistic discernment, then, is a conscious action of the present moment. One good reason I would want to be in continuous discernment is to increase my sensitivity to what the moment is asking.

In classic texts on discernment we hear that we are to test the spirits of the event in question. It is true. Not everything we can do is good to do. Moreover, not everything that goes by the name "good" will necessarily be fruitful for the Kingdom. What is the test of discernment? We sometimes hear that the bottom-line criterion for discernment is *peace.* Often I hear people say, "I took this to discernment, and I am at peace about it." Beware of peace! Peacefulness is *only* a measure of discernment if it is the true self that is peaceful. The peacefulness of ego is never sufficient. If my false self is at peace, it means it is satisfied, and if the ego is satisfied, it has no need to surrender.

Often discerning the present moment is very simple. When we are living consciously, awake to the invitation of grace, our natural response to life will often carry the force of discernment with it. We will respond to the moment with the wisdom born of discipleship. However, sometimes discernment will not be easy. There are literally hundreds of variables surrounding the choices we are called to make. Frequently our choices do not line up clearly as good and bad, right and wrong, healthy and unhealthy, growthful and diminishing. Sometimes their complexity asks us to consider the lesser of two evils, or the better of two goods. And sometimes, while we are indeed called to act in the present moment, we simply recognize that we do not have enough control of events to accurately predict what outcome our choices will bring.

In the midst of these types of unsettling circumstances, is there no foundation upon which our discernment can rest? I believe there is. I believe that when all is said and done, the ultimate criterion for the discernment of spirits is *fruitfulness.* I am called to act toward what is most fruitful for the Kingdom. Does my action further the Reign of God? Which of the many choices that might be open to me will likely bear the most fruit?

It is important to remember that fruitfulness is *not* to be equated with productivity, success, acceptance, progress, or a lack of conflict. In itself, fruitfulness is not measured by "what I want," "what you need," or "what will fulfill me as a person." Fruitfulness is not necessarily an element of what is needed for my happiness or a situation's peaceful resolution, although it might come to be. Fruitfulness is solely intent on what furthers the Reign of God at this moment. As such it is possible that the fruit of an experience will vary from moment to moment, even in very similar circumstances. This is all the more reason why our discernment must be conscious.

"Who, then, is the faithful and wise servant, whom the master has put in charge of the household to distribute to them their food at the proper time?"

(Mt 24:45) To the description of the wise steward that has been evolving through the pages of this book -- one who lives consciously in the moment, free of self-deception, liberated from conditioned enslavement to the false self, able therefore to respond with initiative to the grace offered in the present and willingly undertake the Gospel's call to discipleship -- we can add the possession of a heart discerning of the Reign of God, which enables her or him to seek the Master's will and surrender to it.

SEEK FIRST THE REIGN OF GOD

"Ask and it will be given to you; seek and you will find; knock and the door will be opened to you. For everyone who asks, receives; and the one who seeks, finds; and to the one who knocks, the door will be opened." (Mt 7:7-8)

Being in a process of conversion ultimately means entering into a discipleship that is willing to seek the will of God in all things. The reality is that this is not a burden, for God's will is what is life for us. It is the treasure in the field, and its value has no limit.

Doing the will of God means seeking the Reign at every opportunity. In presenting that basic thought throughout this book, I have by necessity explained what this would involve from a theological basis. In doing this, however, I have attempted to be as practical and concrete as possible. In these last two sections I would like to be even more practical, first, in terms of what the journey of conversion entails for the individual, and second, in terms of some implications for the Church. This practicality is imperative for discipleship, as can be seen in the very first principle of a conversion spirituality.

Conversion must always be concrete. It can never be allowed to exist only as an idea or a theory. As beneficial as ideas and theories are, they must be embodied in real life. This is an incarnational principle. Making conversion concrete is hard to do. It is much easier to think about something than to do it. It is much easier to *talk* about something than to do it. In my work as a spiritual director and as a retreat director I have heard many people say many things -- about what they have decided, about what they have learned, about what they *intend* to do, about what they *must* do -- but ultimately it comes down to the action, down to the doing of it. Every experience of conversion, therefore, must be demonstrable. If I cannot manifest it in terms of an action, a real choice, a concrete move in a clear direction, or a practical consequence, if it has no real bearing in space and time, then it might be a nice idea, but it is not yet an action of conversion.

It follows that *conversion must be holistic.* This also is an incarnational principle. If I am to enter into a process of conversion, then all of me must become involved. Again, anything that stops at an idea is not sufficient. There is no such thing as a theoretical conversion. I must be involved at all levels of my being. The Enneagram uses the image of three centers to explain the human person. We are comprised of an intellectual center, an emotional center, and an instinctual/moving center. The three are in continuous interaction and exchange of energy.

Under the bondage of our primary life distortion, however, one or more of these will be impaired. In this condition the flow of energy is disjointed, and we become stuck in our primary addictive nature. One way of understanding the practical benefits of a conversion and transformation process is the re-establishment of the natural and holy balance that exists between the centers.

Connected with this is the principle that *conversion must always be conscious.* Consciousness could be defined as the appropriate response to the events of my life out of all three centers. When I am in mindless addiction, there are parts of me that are shut down. These parts of me must come awake. Conversion implies freedom and commitment, and these can only be experienced in consciousness. Affirming that grace abounds, still we do not fall into holiness. Holiness is hard won, even as it is freely given.

Therefore, *conversion is a process.* Holiness and transformation are not instantaneous, as much as we would wish them to be. There is a timing that in many ways cannot be rushed. We live in a culture that expects immediate gratification; we should not be surprised that many have made it into a spiritual principle. There is no shortcut. It is not possible to jump ahead. Studying the Enneagram is a good example of this. Many want to learn it quickly, and are distressed to find out how involved it is. (Or worse, many think they have learned it quickly, and feel it is a pretty simple system. It is unfortunate that some of these folks are probably teaching it.) To affirm the process-nature of conversion is to affirm the need for compassion. Often compassion can look like the ability to laugh at ourselves when we are caught in our own foolish patterns of addiction... again.

Finally, *conversion looks like surrender,* and that means that something must be falling away. I am called to know what that means for me at this moment. This principle is fundamental, for it implies that conversion must always embody an action called forth by grace. My surrender can only be to the Reign of God, otherwise it is only deprivation. Deprivation only serves to feed ego, and therefore becomes a subtle form of pride. In deprivation I am still in control; I have lost nothing. On the other hand, a true and legitimate conversion cannot be totally mastered or controlled.

Our inability to control the total process of our conversion suggests a great truth: that even though we are called to seek the Reign of God, ultimately the Reign of God finds us. In the overall process of the spiritual life, contrary to what is our usual experience, we are the junior partners in the joint venture between God and ourselves. In the final analysis it is not possible for us to bring about transformation. It is not like the mixing of a set of chemicals that will inevitably result in a certain product. Even with all the correct ingredients, something more has to happen. While I cannot bring about transformation, however, I can do my best to procure the right ingredients. Or to use the metaphor of a plant, my growth is not in my power, but I can at least prepare the soil so that it is able to support life.

The active part of my seeking the Reign of God, therefore, is a preparation for something I have no control over. It requires that I wait, but my waiting is with a faith that I will be found at the proper time. This preparation, however, is not inconsequential. There are real, concrete things to seek in order to respond fully to the invitation that is offered.

I must *seek honesty.* The spiritual life cannot progress in self-deception. I have to use a ruthless initiative to search out the ways I have been unconsciously fooling myself. I need to seek the *whole* truth. My self-deception continues to thrive as long as I only settle for a partial honesty. Seeking the whole truth will inevitably bring me face to face with my distorted motivational core. This is, of course, an essential beginning. It offers me the possibility of a quantum leap in my conversion process.

Still the need for honesty does not end here. After this I must continue to deal honestly with my *resistances.* Often the most common resistances are experienced by me as events that carry with them various levels of uncomfortability. Again, ego seeks a false peace. I must gradually learn to live in the uncomfortable areas of my life, where I have been fooled into thinking that what is really automatic conditioning is the natural way life is for me. In living honestly, I see that "automatic" and "natural" are not interchangable.

This kind of lived honesty always brings me to the edge, where resistance sets up all sorts of barriers and roadblocks. When I find myself saying, "oh, I can't do that," or "I don't allow myself to get into those situations," I have stumbled upon some kind of resistance. My honesty asks me to explore this resistance. Being at the edge is not in itself devastating, and in fact is often liberating. At the edge is the invitation. If I were to wonder where I might most quickly attain a new level of freedom, it would be at the edge. I will never grow very much while simply walking around within my comfort zone. Holiness lies at the edge of my resistance. Integrally linked with this is the continual need to *seek recognition*. I must desire the ability to spot my motivational core in every one of the hundred ways it manifests itself. Recognizing the mindless and destructive behaviors I have fallen into is the quickest way to proceed with conversion. I must continue to identify the life patterns that point to the presence of unconscious conditioning. I must long to recognize in the experiences of my life the presence of inner disturbances and negative emotion that can point to the distortions of the false self. I must continue to be aware of the feedback I get from others, directly and indirectly, and wish to pursue what this information can reveal about myself and my life choices.

Then, of course, I must *seek freedom*. I must long for the ability to make conscious choices, the kind of choices for what in my experience will bring me to faith, commitment, justice, community, and intimacy. To do this I will have to begin making the necessary connections -- personal, social, and global connections -- that shatter the illusions of the false self. I will have to discern my values, not only to determine which ones are good and useful and which are not, but also simply to recognize which are *mine*. I can only be free in values that I have freely chosen. The very best objective actions can actually frustrate my growth and conversion if they are done out of a motivational script given to me by someone else. It isn't a question of not wanting to act that way; it is a question of wanting to act that way *freely*.

The surest way to seek conversion, in my opinion, is to *seek to live out of my virtuous action*. The Enneagram recognizes that each of the nine spaces on the model possesses a personal life strength. (Of course, in occupying one of these spaces I can *only* possess this virtue to the extent that I live in freedom and consciousness.) An action I undertake in accord with the virtue of my Enneagram life position, when done in honesty, will necessarily be an action of consciousness. I cannot unconsciously practice my virtue, for it always requires a free and conscious choice. When we speak of the nine virtues, we are not speaking of distorted motivation. The virtues are actions of the true self, and they are not conditioned behavior. It might very well be that in time the practice of my virtue could become very natural and spontaneous, but that is a very different reality from mindless conditioning.

I must also *seek the present moment*. The virtue can only be practiced at one place and time, and that is in the *kairos* moment. It is fruitless to regret lost opportunities. It is of little use to waste this moment in needless apprehension. Neither the past nor the future offer any advantage. The bridegroom is coming now. The master is arriving. This moment's yield is ready for the harvest. The time to act is present. The Reign of God is at hand.

Of all the present experiences that are offered to us conceivably the most significant is prayer. Perhaps some readers have wondered why a book on spirituality has said so little about prayer. It is not because prayer is immaterial. Quite the contrary is true. Prayer is, of course, an extremely beneficial and essential aspect of our walk in faith. As an event and experience of our life process, however, prayer possesses the same dynamics as every other life event. What I have said throughout this book applies as much to prayer as to anything else. Prayer is meant to be a freeing and conscious response to God's grace. However, we must realize that unfortunately it is possible for prayer to become one more mindless attempt by the false self to preserve some addictive self-image. Prayer can be as self-serving as anything else. Of course, in that event it is no longer really prayer, but unfortunately we continue to speak of it in the same way -- "my prayer."

On the other hand, my truly free and conscious attempts at prayer possess a tremendous fruitfulness. And prayer can facilitate my journey to freedom and conversion because it has the ability to pull me into the present moment. Prayer is, after all, a conscious attempt to establish and deepen a relationship of mutual presence, a relationship between I as subject and God as subject. This happens at many levels, and more than merely from the intellectual center. My prayer, like the rest of my life, must be holistic.

There are any number of excellent books on prayer, and it would not particularly enhance this book to merely repeat what is included in them. However, it is worth saying that, in my experience, we are *led* in prayer. The Spirit of God guides and directs us. This fundamental belief necessarily qualifies what could be said about prayer styles, methods, and types. There are many excellent methods of prayer, both Western and Eastern, arising from all the human centers -- intellectual, emotional, and instinctual/moving. The method, however, whatever it is, is always secondary. The focus on the presence of God always remains primary. Ultimately I do not pick a prayer method because I am a certain "type." Instead, I use a particular method because the Spirit of God nourishes me through it. When that method ceases to be fruitful, then I have a discernable sign of God leading me toward something else. (Again, fruitfulness is not to be equated with success or consolation. Darkness can be quite fruitful at times.) When I am led to something else I stay with that for as long as it nourishes my journey of faith. It is good and beneficial to experiment with various styles of prayer, but there is never an advantage to adopting a method simply because someone told me that is how I "should" pray.

I do not enter into prayer to seek a utilitarian purpose. I enter into it solely to encounter God. However, prayer does serve the purpose of drawing me into the conscious moment. It shows me what it means to choose to live in a God-consciousness. This is ultimately the same stance I am to take in regard to every event of my life. Paul urges us to "pray without ceasing." (1 Thes 5:17) I am not to go through my day reciting prayers under my breath, but I am to continuously encounter God consciously in the moment.

A final element of preparation in seeking the Reign of God is the need to *seek compassion*. This has already been mentioned, and needs only be reaffirmed here. The wise steward is one who chooses love as the true motive for the spiritual journey. Love, however, is always embodied in some way in truth and compassion. We are constantly being called to seek both at all times. If our love lacks either of these qualities, we run a great risk of manufacturing something else and merely calling it love. If, for instance, my love does not possess truth, I am in danger of sliding into manipulation and the co-dependent mode we sometimes call enabling. If, on the other hand, my love lacks compassion, I can fall into perfectionism, judgmentalism, and violence. These can appear in very subtle forms, and can be extremely hard to find and root out.

The Christian call, from the preaching of Jesus onward, has been to seek compassion. If we as individuals and as a community of faith have failed in our efforts to be disciples of Jesus, it is predominantly here. There are many reasons for this; perhaps the Enneagram would suggest there are nine reasons for it. However, one major reason for our failure to be compassionate is fear. It is most often our feelings of radical mistrust and insecurity that cause us to withhold mercy from our sister or brother. Moreover, the feelings of a lack of worth and mistrust of self can keep us from showing ourselves care and compassion.

As has already been noted, not all of life's experiences are easily discerned, and sometimes it is difficult to know how to balance truth and compassion in the course of our life's circumstances. In many ways the withholding of one can pass as the possession of the other. In the name of compassion I can live for years in a relationship that is self-destructive and dysfunctional. In the name of truth tremendous

harm has been done to countless peop
faith community whose life circumstances ⌐
match the Church's "standards." We must recog-
that, as followers of Jesus, we are called to embrace
both truth and compassion, and that *it is possible* to
do both. We must also recognize that it is likely we
will often fail. Sometimes in our fraility we may have
to come down on one side or the other. It seems to
me that, as disciples of Jesus, if we had to choose, we
would want to err on the side of compassion. While
avoiding manipulation, Jesus always did the compassionate thing. If in doubt we also seek to do the
compassionate thing, we will, at least at a trust level,
be choosing to stand with Jesus.

Seeking the Reign of God is always a matter of
concrete action. If I am seeking honesty, the recognition of sin, the movements of freedom, the pursuit
of virtuous action, a response to the present moment,
and the exercise of compassion, I will be opening
myself to the inbreaking of *kairos*. I wait for grace to
shatter the bounds of my experience. To be the wise
steward I wait with patience and vigilance, ready to
act upon the mysterious and compelling presence of
the Reign of God.

CONVERSION AND THE COMMUNITY OF FAITH

Conversion is never undertaken in isolation. The
call to discipleship is not just given to an individual.
The Church too is called to be a wise steward. The
community of faith actually has a double call. It is,
first of all, called in service to the Kingdom, to invite

and encourage all to embrace the Gospel and undertake conversion. It is also called to respond to the Gospel itself. And in this sense the Church itself must be continally seeking to initiate the process of repentance within itself. These two calls really are one call -- to proclaim in word and deed the coming of the Reign of God.

To fulfill this mission, the community of faith will seek to open itself to the same dynamics that each individual Christian hopes to implement. The Church will be called, for instance, to seek truth and honesty. Part of this will necessarily include Holy Suspicion. In terms of a track record, the Church through the ages has always been more able to call forth truth from the world around it than it has been able to consistently pursue a level of self-honesty. The standards of the world can easily lull to sleep, and the Church is not immune to its song. Justice, equality, openness, unity -- these are values that are easier to hold in theory than to live out in practice. The call to conversion is one that requires the Church to recognize its own potential to fall into consensus trance, and to take steps to again affirm its own free response to the Gospel, as it advocates that response for others.

We have been promised freedom. Jesus says, "...you will know the truth, and the truth will set you free." (John 8:32) It is a freedom connected with the Gospel's power to break through the self-deceptions of the world. Because of our own illusions, the world keeps us in fear. Scripture tells us again and again, "Do not be afraid." Too often we do not believe it, or at least we fail to act upon it. As a Church, as well as individuals, we are not free from fear. Our fear urges us to be protective, to be suspicious, to be judgmental. Whole portions of the wider faith community seek to cling to a security that is born of narrowness. We criticize what we don't understand, and are too threatened to learn. We do these things under the banner of the Kingdom, but the attitudes that are made evident are in reality far from the fruitfulness of the Reign.

To break the bonds of fear, the Church will have to more completely embrace compassion. We can be an extremely compassionate Church, manifesting the resurrected presence of Jesus in the world. There are times, however, when the Church as a body can fall far short of the ministry of compassion witnessed to in the Gospel. Too often the mercy that Jesus brought so freely to others has been sacrificed in the name of perfectionism and law. The basic Christian law is the commandment of love, a love that incarnates the mercy of God.

To embody the compassionate love of God, the Church must continue to surrender to the Spirit's invitation of the present moment. Right now there is a way the Church is called to be in the world. It must seek a discernment that can call that presence forth. Just as the individual Christian does, the Church as a whole must seek discernment. Even with its body of revelation, the Spirit calls the Church to discern how it is to implement that revelation in its contemporary circumstances.

There is a place where honesty, freedom, and compassion come together in the Church, and that is in the sacrament of reconciliation. This is the faith community's locus for conversion, and it is appropriate that the final remarks of this book be addressed to this communal expression of Gospel *metanoia.* Reconciliation is not the same as conversion. Instead it implies an action that follows the individual's commitment to repentance. Once I have seen the need for conversion, and have made the decision to turn my life back to God, then I am ready to seek reconciliation, a reconciliation with God, but also a reconciliation with my brothers and sisters. I am also ready to reconcile with myself.

It is safe to say that within the entire sacramental structure of the Church in our present day, there is no other sacrament that is so misunderstood, so prone to abuse, and so undervalued. There is no other sacrament that is so lacking in sound theological development. There is no other sacrament that can so instill terror in the hearts of the faithful. Is it then any wonder that so many otherwise vibrant and committed Catholics avoid it at any cost? It could well be that the experience of the Church today is suggesting a complete reworking of our understanding of what this sacrament is all about.

By way of definition, *the sacrament of reconciliation is an ecclesial celebration of a moment in the conversion process.* First, it is ecclesial. It is concerned with the Church. It is not about me and God alone. It is not about me and God and a voice behind a screen, or some authority figure I fear will judge me, or the pastor who knows me by name and might think less of me. It is about the faith community having an interest in my transformation, in my journey of the spirit. Perhaps this ecclesial dimension exists between me and one other person (as, for instance, between penitent and confessor), or perhaps it exists within a community context. Either way, I cannot lose sight of the fact that we who celebrate this reconciliation are a manifestation of the faith community, gathered to celebrate my conversion.

It is a celebration, although we might never know it from how the rite is often experienced. In our contemporary experience of the sacrament, frequently neither the priest nor the penitent seem to be much in the mood to celebrate. I wonder sometimes if most Catholics know there is a *new rite* of penance. For many very little has changed (and this too often includes the clergy). The present rite of penance was designed to be less formal, more personal, more open to variation and spontaneity. But if we eliminate the informality, the personal qualities, the variation, the spontaneity, it is true we have a dry shell that looks very much like what we had before. We also run the risk of eliminating the celebration, the opportunity to rejoice in what God's grace is accomplishing, the opportunity to allow the Church to meet an individual believer at a significant moment of life.

The Church is celebrating a moment in an individual's conversion. It is celebrating it, not initiating it. The conversion has already begun. It is that spirit of conversion that has moved the penitent to come in the first place. It is the Spirit of God that initiates conversion. The Church primarily seals the experience that it perceives is already happening. To do this with authenticity, the Church itself must stand "inside" reconciliation. The faith community must acknowledge that it is in need of reconciliation too. If we are not ready and open to ask for reconciliation from God, we have no right to presume to offer it to others.

When the penitent comes for reconciliation it is not enough that he or she wishes to have certain sins forgiven. That is a fine place to start, but is nothing more than the beginning. The Gospel call is not simply to repent. It is to repent and believe in the Good News. The repentance is only the prelude to the radical restructuring of life around discipleship. If all I have is a list of sins, and all the priest has is a formula to remove them, we might have experienced validity, but we have not entered into a celebration of the conversion process.

This implies that the penitent comes seeking a *direction*. The sacrament is about conversion, transformation, and reconciliation. These all imply that I have entered a process that wishes to move me in a concrete path. I have a destination. To move toward this destination, it is essential that I get to the level of motivation. If I cannot seek out the roots of my sinfulness, I am probably doomed to continue in the same rut. The problem with what some have called the "shopping list" of sins is that they really insulate me from real change. I become used to them, and they in turn can buffer me from truly exploring the ways I am bound up and enslaved.

If the Church, however, asks the penitent to move away from the stock list of sins, and catechizes the faithful to a new level of appreciation for the sacrament, then it had better also change its ideas about how the sacrament is ministered. Leaving aside the whole issue of communal penance, and looking only at individual, private reconciliation, we discover that in the usual way the sacrament is offered, there is little room to enter into a deeper motivational and attitudinal exploration of sinfulness. Most confessors structure reconciliation in such a way that deviation from the set pattern would clearly be discouraged, or even simply not tolerated. Many confessors, in fact, would feel extremely inadequate entering into areas "reserved" for spiritual direction or pastoral counseling.

The Church, then, needs ministers of reconciliation who are willing and able to bring a new attitude to the sacrament of reconciliation. They must be people attuned to listening to another's story, and able to offer from their own faith and from their own store of experience any help necessary in searching out the new directions of conversion and transformation the penitent is seeking. They must be ministers who can journey with another, being willing to act as a companion on a path that sometimes is dark, sometimes scary, sometimes fantastically brilliant. And they must be willing to enter into a celebration, taking the time necessary to give the appropriate honor and care for an individual's experiences.

This celebration of the sacrament is in fact already a frequent occurrence in some circles in the Church. It is also capable of being implemented even now at a much wider range within the faith community. It does not need legislation, for that is already there. It needs education, commitment, and an initiative that itself is born of a conversion process -- a conversion process of the Church as a whole, a coming to maturity in our understanding of the journey of faith, a willingness to enter further into the mystery of discipleship.

What can the Enneagram offer to this kind of sacramental celebration? First, the very fact that it can be a significant tool in an individual's conversion process will itself benefit the sacramental process. Second, as a call to freedom and consciousness, it will challenge the faith community to continuously place the sacrament within a context of individual, ecclesial, and global liberation. Third, it will provide a motivational basis for the Church's encounter with the penitent. Because of this, it will be less likely that either the individual or the community will be able to resist conversion by focusing solely on acts and avoiding deeper implications. Fourth, it will enable the faith community to itself remain within a conversion process. Rather than meeting the penitent with condescension, therefore, it will ask the Church to approach reconciliation as a mutual exchange of grace.

By way of conclusion, it is worth noting that the Enneagram is *always* an option -- for the individual and for the faith community alike. Like so many other beneficial spiritual tools present to us, each of us can choose whether to pursue the Enneagram or not. It is not mandatory. There are, however, some things that are. The Gospel is not optional. Conversion is not optional if we wish to be disciples of Jesus. A present response to the Reign of God is not optional if we truly seek to do God's will.

I have attempted to present the Enneagram as a tool that can further conversion, but I also urge anyone who finds it a burden to let it go. There is no spiritual tool that is so important that it must be allowed to become a stumbling block to the spiritual journey. For those who have found it helpful, or even pivotal to their conversion, I urge them to move beyond an informational level, and explore more deeply the experiential level. There comes a point where more information becomes counterproductive. It gives the illusion one is progressing, when in fact there might be little substantive transformation. It will be in the experiences of life that grace will be found. We are called to be wise -- certainly not in our own estimation, but in our use of what is offered to us by the Spirit of God.

FURTHER READING SUGGESTIONS

The following works are provided in order that the reader might pursue further some of the ideas presented in this book. They are offered either as background resources (scriptural or theological) or as works that speak to various aspects of conversion or transformation.

Beesing, Maria, Robert J. Nogosek, and Patrick H. O'Leary. *The Enneagram: A Journey of Self Discovery.* Denville, NJ: Dimension Books, 1984.

Bennett, J.G. *The Sevenfold Work.* Charles Town, WV: Claymont Communications, 1979.

_____. *Transformation.* Charles Town, WV: Claymont Communications, 1978.

Boadt, Lawrence. *Reading the Old Testament.* New York: Paulist Press, 1984.

Conn, Walter E., ed. *Conversion: Perspectives on Personal and Social Transformation.* New York: Alba House, 1978.

Crosby, Michael H. *Spirituality of the Beatitudes: Matthew's Challenge for First World Christians.* Maryknoll, NY: Orbis Books, 1981.

Edwards, Tilden. *Living Simply Through the Day.* New York: Paulist Press, 1977.

Ellis, Peter F. *The Genius of John: A Composition-Critical Commentary on the Fourth Gospel.* Collegeville, MN: The Liturgical Press, 1984.

Feinstein, David, and Stanley Krippner. *Personal Mythology: The Psychology of Your Evolving Self.* Los Angeles: Jeremy P. Tarcher, Inc., 1988.

Fox, Matthew. *Original Blessing: A Primer In Creation Spirituality.* Sante Fe, NM: Bear & Company, Inc., 1983.

Galipeau, Steven A. *Transforming Body and Soul; Therapeutic Wisdom in the Gospel Healing Stories.* New York: Paulist Press, 1990.

Gurdjieff, G.I. *Meetings with Remarkable Men.* New York: E.P. Dutton, 1974.

Haughton, Rosemary. *The Transformation of Man: A Study of Conversion and Community.* Springfield, IL: Templegate, 1967.

Ichazo, Oscar. *Between Metaphysics and Protoanalysis: A Theory for Analyzing the Human Psyche.* New York: Arica Institute Press, 1982.

Johnson, Elizabeth A. *Consider Jesus: Waves of Renewal In Christology.* New York: Crossroad, 1990.

Kelley, Mary Helen. *Skin Deep (Designer Clothes by God).* Memphis: Monastery of St. Clare, 1990.

Keyes, Margaret Frings. *Emotions and the Enneagram.* Muir Beach, CA: Molysdatur Publications, 1990.

Lifton, Robert Jay. *The Broken Connection; On Death and the Continuity of Life.* New York: Basic Books, Inc., 1983.

McCormick, Patrick. *Sin as Addiction.* New York: Paulist Press, 1989.

McNeill, Donald P., Douglas A. Morrison, and Henri J. M. Nouwen. *Compassion: A Reflection on the Christian Life.* Garden City, New York: Image, 1982.

Martos, Joseph. *Doors to the Sacred.* Garden City, New York: Image, 1982.

Metz, Barbara, and John Burchill. *The Enneagram and Prayer*. Denville, NJ: Dimension Books, 1987.

Miller, David L. *Christs: Meditations on Archetypal Images in Christian Theology*. New York: The Seabury Press, 1981.

Moore, Sebastian. *The Crucified Jesus Is No Stranger*. New York: The Seabury Press, 1977.

Nicoll, Maurice. *Psychological Commentaries on the Teaching of Gurdjieff and Ouspensky*. Boulder: Shambhala, 1984.

Nogosek, Robert J. *Nine Portraits of Jesus: Discovering Jesus Through the Enneagram*. Denville, NJ: Dimension Books, 1987.

Ouspensky, Peter D. *In Search of the Miraculous*. New York and London: Harcourt, Brace, Jovanovich, 1977.

Palmer, Helen. *The Enneagram: Understanding Yourself and the Others in Your Life*. San Francisco: Harper & Row, Publishers, 1988.

Peck, M. Scott. *The People of the Lie*. New York: Simon & Schuster, 1983.

Perkins, Pheme. *Reading the New Testament*. New York: Paulist Press, 1988.

Riso, Don Richard. *Personality Types: Using the Enneagram for Self-Discovery*. Boston: Houghton Mifflin Company, 1987.

_____. *Understanding the Enneagram: The Practical Guide to Personality Types*. Boston: Houghton Mifflin Company, 1990.

Schillebeeckx, Edward. *Christ: The Experience of Jesus as Lord*. New York: The Seabury Press, 1980.

_____. *Jesus: An Experiment in Christology.* New York: The Seabury Press, 1979.

Shah, Idries. *Tales of the Dervishes.* New York: E. P. Dutton, 1967.

_____. *Wisdom of the Idiots.* London: The Octagon Press, 1969.

Speeth, Kathleen Riordan. *The Gurdjieff Work.* New York: Pocket Books, Simon & Schuster, 1976.

Tart, Charles T., ed. *Transpersonal Psychologies.* New York, San Francisco, et al: Harper & Row, 1975.

_____. *Waking Up: Overcoming the Obstacles To Human Potential.* Boston: New Science Library, Shambhala, 1986.

Wallis, James. *The Call To Conversion.* San Francisco: Harper & Row, 1981.ed.